Collins

Easy Learning

GCSE Higher

science

Exam Practice Workbook

FOR AQA A + B

Contents

Coordination

1 a The diagram shows a neurone from the human body.

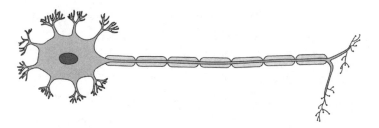

    i What type of neurone is this? _____ [1 mark]

    ii Draw an arrow on the diagram to show the direction in which the nerve
impulse travels along the neurone. [1 mark]

b In what form does the nerve impulse travel along the neurone?

_____ [1 mark]

Receptors

2 If you touch a very hot object, you react by moving your hand away very quickly.

a Name the receptor and effector in this response.

Receptor _____ Effector _____ [2 marks]

b Receptors transform one form of energy into another. Name the **two** forms of
energy in this response.

The receptor transforms _____ energy to

_____ energy. [2 marks]

3 a Adrenaline is secreted by the adrenal glands when you get a sudden fright.
It makes the heart beat faster.

    i Name the target organ of adrenaline.

_____ [1 mark]

    ii Suggest how adrenaline could help you to escape from danger.

_____ [1 mark]

b Describe **two** ways in which transmitting information using hormones differs
from transmitting information using neurones.

1 _____

2 _____ [2 marks]

Reflex actions

1 a The diagram shows a synapse.

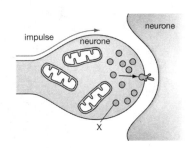

    i What is contained in the structure labelled X? _____ [1 mark]

    ii Describe how the nerve impulse travels across the synapse.

    _____

    _____ [2 marks]

b Adam puts his hand onto a pin. A sensory neurone carries an impulse to his central nervous system, where the impulse is passed on to a motor neurone.

    i How many synapses are there in this pathway? _____ [1 mark]

    ii Suggest **one** advantage of having synapses in pathways such as this.

    _____ [1 mark]

In control

2 a Sports drinks usually contain glucose, sodium ions and chloride ions.
Explain why an athlete might need to take in extra sodium and chloride ions.

_____

_____ [2 marks]

b If you have too much glucose in your blood, your pancreas secretes a hormone called insulin. Describe how insulin helps to make the blood glucose level go back to normal.

_____

_____ [2 marks]

c i Jill has diabetes. Her pancreas does not secrete insulin. Suggest why Jill's body may run out of glucose if she does not eat carbohydrate-containing foods at regular intervals.

_____

_____ [2 marks]

ii Explain why it is dangerous for the body to run out of glucose.

_____

_____ [2 marks]

Reproductive hormones

1 a The flow diagram shows how three hormones help to control the menstrual cycle.

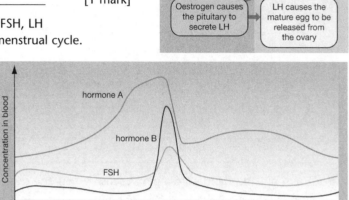

i Name the gland that secretes FSH and LH.

_____ [1 mark]

ii Name the gland that secretes oestrogen.

_____ [1 mark]

b The graph shows how the levels of FSH, LH and oestrogen change during the menstrual cycle.

i On the graph, use an arrow to show when ovulation is most likely to occur.

[1 mark]

ii During which days is menstruation most likely to occur? [1 mark]

iii Name hormones A and B.

A _____

B _____

[2 marks]

Controlling fertility

2 This table shows the success rate for one IVF treatment in women of different ages.

Age of woman in years	Chance of having a baby after IVF
23–35	More than 20%
36–38	15%
39	10%
40 and over	Less than 6%

a Describe how a woman's age affects the success rate for IVF treatment.

_____ [1 mark]

b Using the data in the table, and your own ideas, suggest arguments supporting the idea that women over 55 years of age should not be given IVF treatment on the National Health Service.

_____

_____ [2 marks]

3 FSH may be given to women whose eggs do not mature naturally, to help them to conceive. This treatment often results in multiple births. Suggest an explanation for this.

_____

_____ [2 marks]

Diet and energy

1 a Katie has a high metabolic rate. Olivia's metabolic rate is lower. Olivia is jealous of Katie because Katie can eat more food than Olivia without putting on weight.

   i What is **metabolic rate**?

_____ [1 mark]

   ii Explain why Katie's high metabolic rate means that she can eat more food than Olivia without putting on weight.

_____

_____ [2 marks]

   iii Suggest what Olivia could do to increase her metabolic rate.

_____ [1 mark]

b Carbohydrate, fat and protein are the three nutrients that provide us with energy.

   i Which of these three nutrients contains the most energy per gram?

_____ [1 mark]

   ii Describe how body cells release energy from carbohydrate.

_____

_____ [2 marks]

Obesity

2 The graph shows the percentage of obese men and women in five different countries.

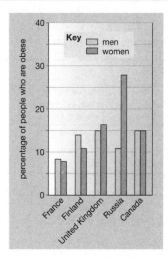

a In what way does the pattern of obesity in Russia differ from the pattern in Canada?

_____ [1 mark]

b Lisa says that the pattern of obesity in Russia suggests that it is caused by a person's eating and exercise habits, rather than by their genes. Explain how the data supports this view.

_____

_____ [2 marks]

c Explain why obese people are more likely to suffer from arthritis than people of normal weight.

_____

_____ [2 marks]

Not enough food

1 a A slimming programme advertises that you can lose 18 lbs (8 kg) in four days. It says:

> The 18-in-4 programme identifies common, but specific FRUITS, VEGETABLES, CHICKEN AND BEEF that need to be eaten in specific combinations. These combinations of specific foods work with the body's chemistry and result in accelerated weight loss.

i Explain why the **combination** of food that a person eats, rather than the **quantity** of food that they eat, is unlikely to help them lose weight.

_____ [1 mark]

ii Suggest **two** reasons why it is not good for a person to lose this much weight so quickly if they are trying to improve their health.

1 _____

2 _____ [2 marks]

iii In 2005, a slimming diet that involved eating mostly proteins and fats, with no carbohydrate, was very popular. Explain why this diet could increase the risk of developing heart disease.

_____

_____ [2 marks]

D–C

B–A*

Cholesterol and salt

2 This table shows information about the cholesterol concentration in the blood of men and women in two cities in the United Kingdom. A blood cholesterol concentration above 6.6 units is dangerous to health.

City	Men		Women	
	Average cholesterol concentration	Percentage with cholesterol above 6.6 units	Average cholesterol concentration	Percentage with cholesterol above 6.6 units
A	5.9	27	5.9	31
B	6.1	35	6.1	36

a What conclusion can be drawn from this data?

A Men have a higher risk of developing heart disease than women.

B People in City A eat more fat than people in City B.

C People in City B have a higher risk of developing heart disease than people in City A.

D Women eat more fat than men. [1 mark]

b Suggest how this data should have been collected in order to make a fair comparison between City A and City B.

_____

_____ [2 marks]

c The liver makes cholesterol when blood cholesterol levels are low. Drugs called statins inhibit the enzyme that makes cholesterol. Suggest why taking statins can reduce blood cholesterol levels more than can be done by changing your diet.

_____

_____ [2 marks]

D–C

B–A*

Drugs

1 a Explain what is meant by being **addicted** to a drug.

_____

_____ [2 marks]

b Cocaine is an illegal and very addictive drug. This graph shows the percentage of people between 16 and 29 and between 30 and 59 who told researchers that they took cocaine in 2006. In each age group, people are grouped according to how often they visit nightclubs.

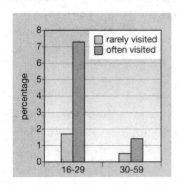

i Compare the percentages of the frequent nightclub visitors in the two age groups who reported taking cocaine in 2006.

_____

_____ [2 marks]

ii Describe the relationship between visiting nightclubs and taking cocaine, as shown by this data.

_____

_____ [2 marks]

Trialling drugs

2 This table shows the results of a trial to test a new drug to help people to recover from flu.

		Given zanamivir	Given a placebo
A	Mean age of subjects in years	19	19
B	Number of days until their temperature went down to normal	2.00	2.33
C	Number of days until they lost all their symptoms and felt better	3.00	3.83
D	Number of days until they felt just as well as before they had flu	4.5	6.3
E	Average score the volunteers gave to their experience of the five major symptoms of flu	23.4	25.3

Answer these questions using information in the table.

a Give the letter of the row in the table that shows how the researchers kept one variable constant in their trial. _____ [1 mark]

b Give the letters of **all** the rows in the table that show that the drug helps people to get over flu more quickly.

_____ [1 mark]

c The trial was a **double-blind** trial. What does this mean?

A Both the researchers and the subjects know who is being given the drug or placebo.

B Neither the subjects nor the researchers know who is being given the drug or a placebo.

C Only the researchers know whether which subjects are being given the drug or a placebo.

D Only the subjects know whether they are being given the drug or a placebo. [1 mark]

d Despite extensive trials such as this one, some new drugs have unexpected side effects when they are in general use. Suggest why these side effects are not discovered during the trials.

_____

_____ [2 marks]

Illegal drugs

1 a Explain how injecting heroin into the blood can increase the risk of getting HIV/AIDS.

_____

_____ [2 marks]

b Explain why people who have begun taking cocaine may find it almost impossible to stop taking the drug.

_____

_____ [2 marks]

Alcohol

2 The table shows the number of people who were admitted to hospital in one area of the USA in one year because they had been taking drugs.

Drug they had taken	Number of men admitted to hospital	Number of women admitted to hospital
Alcohol	380	140
Heroin and similar drugs	90	50
Cocaine	40	30
Cannabis	100	20

a What does this data show?

A Alcohol causes more hospital admissions than heroin.

B Heroin is more dangerous than cocaine.

C More men than women drink alcohol.

D More people use cannabis than heroin. [1 mark]

b Zachary says that the table shows that more men than women take these drugs. Is he right? Explain your answer.

_____

_____ [2 marks]

c Excessive drinking of alcohol damages the liver. Why does this happen?

_____ [1 mark]

d Explain how this data supports the statement that the overall impact of legal drugs on health is greater than the impact of illegal drugs.

_____

_____ [2 marks]

Tobacco

1 This graph shows information about the numbers of men who smoked and the numbers of men who died of lung cancer between 1911 and 2001.

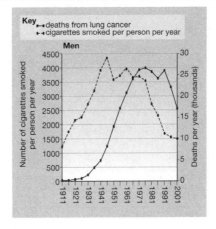

a Using the information on the graph, suggest why it was not until the 1950s that it was recognised that smoking could be causing cancer.

_____

_____ [2 marks]

b The data in the graph shows a correlation between smoking and lung cancer. Explain why this does not prove that smoking causes lung cancer.

_____ [1 mark]

c Tobacco smoke contains carbon monoxide. Explain how this can reduce the birth weight of a baby born to a woman who smokes during pregnancy.

_____

_____

_____ [3 marks]

Pathogens

2 a What is a pathogen?

A An infectious disease.

B A microorganism that causes disease.

C An organism that transmits disease.

D A gene that causes inherited disease. [1 mark]

b Ignaz Semmelweis worked in labour wards in Austria in the 1840s. Describe how he helped to reduce the death rate of women who gave birth there.

_____

_____ [2 marks]

c Even today there are still serious problems with the spread of infections in hospitals. Suggest why these problems are greater in hospitals than in other places.

_____

_____ [2 marks]

Body defences

1 The diagrams show a cell attacking a bacterium.

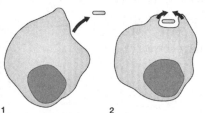

1   2   3

a What is the name for this process?

_____ [1 mark]

b Describe what happens to the bacterium after the cell has surrounded it.

_____

_____ [2 marks]

D–C

2 This table shows the total number of people in the world who suffered from the new infectious disease, SARS, in February and March 2003.

Country	Number of cases of SARS
China	95
Viet Nam	40
Singapore	20
Canada	2
Switzerland	1
Thailand	1

a How could SARS have spread from China, Viet Nam and Singapore to Canada and Switzerland?

_____

_____ [2 marks]

b Explain how the table suggests that this outbreak of SARS was an epidemic, rather than a pandemic.

_____

_____ [2 marks]

B–A*

Drugs against disease

3 a Drug companies have not been very successful in finding effective antiviral drugs. What helps to explain this?

A Viruses are too small to see.

B Viruses are too dangerous for researchers to work with.

C Viruses reproduce inside body cells.

D Viruses reproduce very slowly. [1 mark]

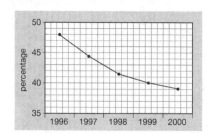

b This graph shows the percentage of children between the ages of 0 and 4 who were prescribed antibiotics each year between 1996 and 2000 in the USA.
  i By how much did antibiotic prescriptions for this group of children fall between 1996 and 2000?

_____ [1 mark]

  ii Explain why it is important to try to reduce the number of antibiotic prescriptions.

_____

_____ [2 marks]

D–C

B–A*

Arms race

1 Most deaths from MRSA happen in hospitals. Which **cannot** help to explain this?

A A lot of antibiotics are used in hospitals, increasing the chance of antibiotic resistance developing.

B It is easy for bacteria such as MRSA to spread from one person to another in a hospital ward.

C Many people in hospital are already ill and weak.

D MRSA is only found in hospitals.

[1 mark]

2 *Escherichia coli* is a bacterium that can cause infections of the blood and cerebrospinal fluid (the fluid inside the brain and spinal cord). This graph shows the percentage of these infections in the United Kingdom that were caused by strains of *E. coli* that were resistant to the antibiotic ciprofloxacin in the years from 1990 to 2004.

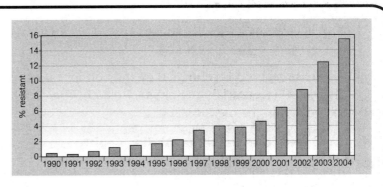

a Describe the trend in antibiotic resistance in *E. coli* between 1990 and 2004.

_____

_____ [2 marks]

b Suggest how this antibiotic resistance has come about.

_____

_____ [2 marks]

Vaccination

3 TB is an infectious disease caused by a bacterium. A vaccine called BCG was introduced in 1951. It is given to most school pupils between the ages of 10 to 14. The table shows the number of new cases of TB in the United Kingdom in some of the years between 1950 and 1990.

Year	Number of new cases of TB
1950	50 000
1960	25 000
1970	16 000
1980	9000
1990	6000

a Do the figures in the table prove that the BCG vaccination has been effective? Explain your answer.

_____

_____ [2 marks]

b Suggest why the number of new cases of TB took many years to drop as low as 6000 cases per year.

_____

_____ [2 marks]

c The TB vaccine contains an extract made from the bacteria that cause TB. Explain how the vaccine can make a person immune to TB.

_____

_____

_____

_____ [4 marks]

B1a revision checklist

I know:

how human bodies respond to changes inside them and to their environment

☐ nerves and hormones coordinate body activities and help control water, ion and blood sugar levels and temperature

☐ receptors transform energy from stimuli into electrical impulses, enabling information to travel rapidly along the nerves

☐ reflex actions are automatic and very fast; they involve sensory, relay and motor neurones, with synapses between them, in a reflex arc

☐ the menstrual cycle is controlled by the hormones oestrogen (secreted by the ovaries), FSH and LH (secreted by the pituitary gland). The concentrations of these hormones change during the menstrual cycle

what we can do to keep our bodies healthy

☐ a healthy diet contains the right balance of the different foods you need and the right amount of energy

☐ obesity increases the risk of arthritis, diabetes, high blood pressure and heart disease

☐ too much cholesterol in the form of LDL in the blood increases the risk of heart disease

☐ the liver makes cholesterol if intake is too low

how we use/abuse medical and recreational drugs

☐ drugs affect people's behaviour and can damage the brain, and some hard drugs (heroin) are addictive. Some drugs are legal (alcohol) and some are illegal (cocaine, heroin)

☐ the substances in tobacco smoke cause many diseases, e.g. cancer and bronchitis

☐ alcohol is a depressant and hinders the activity of parts of the brain

☐ medical drugs are beneficial, but must be thoroughly tested before use

what causes infectious diseases and how our bodies defend themselves against them

☐ pathogenic microorganisms cause infectious diseases

☐ some white blood cells (phagocytes) ingest pathogens and kill them; and others (lymphocytes) make antibodies

☐ antibiotics kill bacteria inside the body but do not kill viruses; however, some bacteria can develop resistance to antibiotics

☐ immunisations and vaccinations offer protection from various diseases

Hot and cold

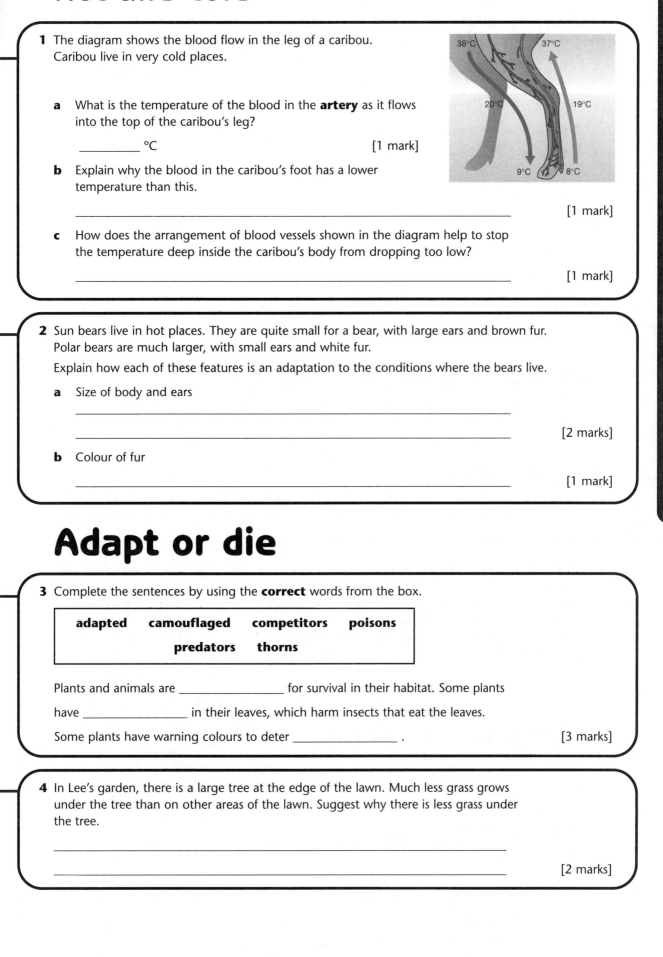

1 The diagram shows the blood flow in the leg of a caribou.
Caribou live in very cold places.

a What is the temperature of the blood in the **artery** as it flows
into the top of the caribou's leg?

_____ °C [1 mark]

b Explain why the blood in the caribou's foot has a lower
temperature than this.

_____

[1 mark]

c How does the arrangement of blood vessels shown in the diagram help to stop
the temperature deep inside the caribou's body from dropping too low?

_____

[1 mark]

2 Sun bears live in hot places. They are quite small for a bear, with large ears and brown fur.
Polar bears are much larger, with small ears and white fur.

Explain how each of these features is an adaptation to the conditions where the bears live.

a Size of body and ears

_____

_____

[2 marks]

b Colour of fur

_____

[1 mark]

Adapt or die

3 Complete the sentences by using the **correct** words from the box.

adapted   camouflaged   competitors   poisons
predators   thorns

Plants and animals are _____ for survival in their habitat. Some plants

have _____ in their leaves, which harm insects that eat the leaves.

Some plants have warning colours to deter _____ . [3 marks]

4 In Lee's garden, there is a large tree at the edge of the lawn. Much less grass grows
under the tree than on other areas of the lawn. Suggest why there is less grass under
the tree.

_____

_____

[2 marks]

Two ways to reproduce

1 a The diagram shows what happens during sexual reproduction.

Match statements, **A**, **B**, **C** and **D**, with the labels **1 – 4** in the diagram.

A This is a female gamete.

B The new cell contains genes from both parents.

C Two gametes fuse together.

D This is a male gamete.

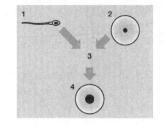

1	2	3	4

[4 marks]

D–C

2 Explain why asexual reproduction produces clones, but sexual reproduction does not.

_____

_____

_____

[2 marks]

B–A*

Genes and what they do

3 a Where in a cell is DNA found?

_____   [1 mark]

b Describe the function of DNA in a cell.

_____

_____   [2 marks]

D–C

4 Snuppy was the first cloned dog. Some egg cells were taken from a female Afghan hound and their nuclei were removed. Some other cells were taken from a male Afghan hound's ear. An egg cell was fused with an ear cell. This formed a 'zygote', which grew into Snuppy.

a Would Snuppy be a clone of the female or the male dog? Explain your answer.

_____

_____   [2 marks]

b Dogs have 78 chromosomes.

i How many chromosomes would there have been in the egg cell taken from the female dog?

_____   [1 mark]

ii How many chromosomes would there have been in the ear cell taken from the male dog?

_____   [1 mark]

iii How many chromosomes are there in each of Snuppy's cells?

_____   [1 mark]

B–A*

Cuttings

D–C

1 Oak trees reproduce sexually. They produce seeds called acorns. Two acorns from an oak tree grow into new trees. One of the trees is much taller than the other.

a Suggest **two** reasons why one tree is taller than the other.

1_____

2_____ [2 marks]

b Gardeners can also grow new trees from cuttings. They take a small piece of stem from a tree and place it in soil. The piece of stem grows roots and becomes a new plant. Mia wants to grow an oak tree exactly like one she already has in her garden. Explain why using cuttings would be better than planting acorns.

_____

_____ [2 marks]

B–A*

2 Banana plants are unable to reproduce sexually.

a Suggest how banana growers can produce new banana plants.

A by sowing seeds

B by taking cuttings

C by crossing one plant with another

D by introducing insects to pollinate the flowers [1 mark]

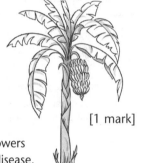

b A disease is killing banana plants. Explain why it is difficult for banana growers to produce a new variety of banana plants that are resistant to this new disease.

_____

_____ [2 marks]

Clones

D–C

3 This diagram shows how new cattle can be produced using a technique called **embryo transplants**.

a Explain why the embryos that are transplanted into the replacement mothers are clones.

_____

_____

_____

_____

_____ [2 marks]

B–A*

b Suggest how this technique could help to save a rare species of animal from extinction.

_____

_____

_____

_____ [2 marks]

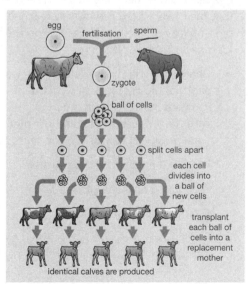

Genetic engineering

1 Read this article about genetically engineered maize.

> Maize seeds are a protein- and carbohydrate-rich food. Maize is grown in many parts of the world. Insect pests reduce yields of maize. Many farmers spray the maize plants with pesticides to kill the pests.
>
> Now some new varieties of maize plants have been produced using genetic engineering. A gene for making a toxin has been transferred into the maize cells. The plants make a toxin (poison) in their leaves, which kills any insects that eat them.

a Explain how the genetically engineered maize could be an **advantage** to each of the following:

i a farmer

_____ [1 mark]

ii a person buying food made with the maize

_____ [1 mark]

b Suggest why some people may not want to eat foods made from genetically modified maize.

_____

_____ [2 marks]

---

2 The diagram shows how genetic engineering has been used to produce insulin from bacteria.

Explain why the insulin that the bacteria make is exactly the same as the insulin made by human cells.

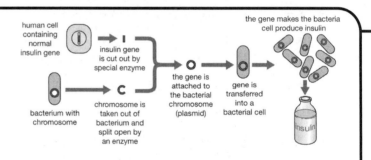

human cell containing normal insulin gene

insulin gene is cut out by special enzyme

the gene is attached to the bacterial chromosome (plasmid)

gene is transferred into a bacterial cell

the gene makes the bacteria cell produce insulin

insulin

bacterium with chromosome

chromosome is taken out of bacterium and split open by an enzyme

_____

_____ [2 marks]

Theories of evolution

3 The drawings show how Lamarck thought that giraffes evolved their long necks. He thought that their necks stretched as they reached for high-up leaves. The giraffes passed on their long necks to their offspring.

a Charles Darwin thought that there was a different explanation. He suggested that there was natural variation in neck length amongst giraffes. The ones with the longest necks could get more food, so they were most likely to survive and reproduce.

What is the name for this process?

A acquired characteristics   **B** extinction

C natural selection   **D** speciation   [1 mark]

b Explain how the process suggested by Darwin could eventually produce a population of giraffes all with long necks.

_____

_____ [2 marks]

Natural selection

1 Peppered moths have pale wings with dark speckles. This camouflages them against tree bark so they are less likely to be eaten by birds. In the industrial revolution, air pollution made tree bark darker. A variety of peppered moths with dark wings became more common than the pale moths.

   a What is the term for the relationship between the birds and the moths?

     A camouflage   **B** competition   **C** evolution   **D** predation   **[1 mark]**

   b What can explain the dark moths becoming more common?

     A Any moths that had dark wings were more likely to survive.

     B The moths changed their colour so that they were better camouflaged from birds.

     C The pale peppered moths flew away to less polluted areas.

     D The polluted air made the moth's wings darker.   **[1 mark]**

   c In the 1950s, the air became much cleaner. Suggest what would have happened to the peppered moth population and explain your suggestion.

     _____

     _____

     _____   **[3 marks]**

2 Species of organisms that live on remote islands are often different from related species that live on the mainland. Suggest why.

   _____

   _____   **[2 marks]**

Fossils and evolution

3 The diagram shows some horses that lived long ago.

   a How do we know about the structure of the legs of horses that lived millions of years ago?

     _____

     _____

     _____ **[1 mark]**

Years ago	What it looked like and idea of size	Bones of its front leg	How it lived
10 million	height: 1.0 m 	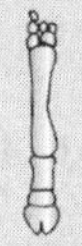	lived in very dry places; it was a fast runner
40 million	height: 0.6 m 	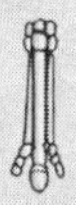	lived in dryer conditions; needed to be able to run away from predators
60 million	height: 0.4 m 		lived on soft ground near water; its feet could support its weight without sinking into the mud

   b Use the theory of natural selection, and the information in the diagram, to suggest why the feet of horses that lived 40 million years ago had three toes but the feet of horses that lived 10 million years ago had only one toe.

     _____

     _____   **[2 marks]**

   c Explain why we cannot conclude that the first or second species of horses shown in the diagram are ancestors of the third species.

     _____

     _____   **[2 marks]**

Extinction

1 Crayfish live in streams and rivers in England. A larger species of crayfish has been introduced from America. The introduced species eats the same food as the English crayfish. It carries a disease that does not affect it but that kills English crayfish.

Explain why the English crayfish may become extinct.

_____

_____

_____

[3 marks]

D–C

2 Dodos were huge, flightless birds that lived on Mauritius, in the Indian Ocean. There were no predators on Mauritius. Dodos became extinct after people arrived on the island.

Suggest why the dodos became extinct.

_____

_____

[2 marks]

B–A*

More people, more problems

3 a The graph shows how the human population has changed since 1750.

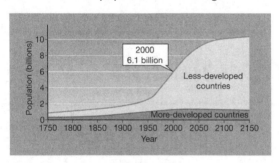

i Which part of the graph is a **prediction**?

_____ [1 mark]

ii How many people lived on Earth in 1920?

_____ [1 mark]

iii By how many times did the world population increase between 1920 and the year 2000?

    A 2   **B** 3   **C** 4   **D** 5   [1 mark]

b List **three** ways in which an increase in the human population reduces the amount of land available for other species.

1 _____

2 _____

3 _____ [3 marks]

c Explain why the human population has grown so rapidly during the 19th and 20th centuries.

_____

_____ [2 marks]

D–C

B–A*

Land use

1 The graph shows an area of land in the United Kingdom that was used for different types of agriculture between 1968 and 2005.

a What can be concluded about changes in the total area of agricultural land between 1986 and 2005?

A It decreased greatly.

B It increased a little.

C It stayed approximately the same.

D We cannot tell because the data does not give enough information.

[1 mark]

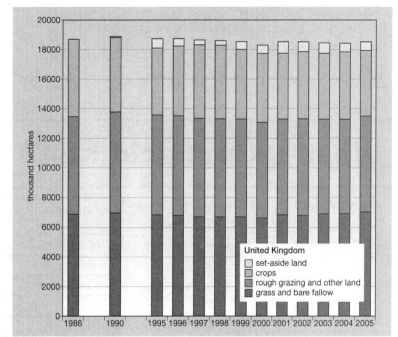

United Kingdom
☐ set-aside land
▨ crops
▨ rough grazing and other land
▨ grass and bare fallow

b Set-aside land is land on which farmers do not grow crops. Farmers are given grants to leave some of their land as set-aside. This is to avoid having too many food crops produced in the European Union which would reduce their price.

i Describe the changes in the area of set-aside land between 1986 and 2005.

_____

_____

[2 marks]

ii Use the graph to suggest which type of land has provided most of the set-aside land.

_____

[1 mark]

iii Suggest how set-aside land could increase biodiversity on farmland.

_____

_____

[2 marks]

Pollution

2 DDT is a persistent insecticide. It does not break down inside the bodies of animals and plants. The diagram shows what happens as DDT passes along a food chain.

a How does the information in the diagram explain why animals at the top of food chains are more likely to be poisoned by DDT than other animals?

_____

_____

_____

[2 marks]

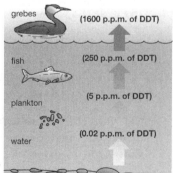

grebes (1600 p.p.m. of DDT)

fish (250 p.p.m. of DDT)

(5 p.p.m. of DDT)

plankton

(0.02 p.p.m. of DDT)

water

b DDT is now banned in Europe and America but DDT is still found in small amounts in animals' bodies. Suggest why this is so.

_____

_____

[2 marks]

Air pollution

1 Sulfur dioxide is a pollutant.
  a Where does most sulfur dioxide come from?

  _____

  [1 mark]

  b Describe **one** way in which sulfur dioxide in the air can damage a person's health.

  _____

  [1 mark]

What causes acid rain?

2 The table shows the pollutants emitted in car exhausts in the United Kingdom in one year.

Pollutant	Emissions in thousands of tonnes
Carbon monoxide	3300
Carbon dioxide	31 200
Smoke particles	130
Nitrogen oxides	714
Sulfur dioxide	12

  a Carbon monoxide combines irreversibly with haemoglobin in our blood. Why is this dangerous?

    A It makes it difficult for oxygen to diffuse into the blood from the lungs.

    B It makes it difficult to breathe.

    C It makes it difficult to supply enough oxygen to respiring cells.

    D It makes it difficult to remove carbon dioxide from the blood.

    [1 mark]

  b Explain how breathing in smoke particles can damage health.

  _____

  [1 mark]

  c Nitrogen oxides and sulfur dioxides both contribute to the formation of acid rain. Describe how acid rain is formed.

  _____

  _____

  [2 marks]

  d Describe **two** harmful effects of acid rain on living organisms.

    1_____

    2_____

    [2 marks]

  e Explain how adding a base, such as limestone, to acidified lakes can help to reduce the harmful effects on wildlife.

  _____

  _____

  [2 marks]

  f The table shows the mass of nitrogen oxides, in thousands of tonnes, that were emitted in exhausts from road vehicles between 1970 and 2005.

Year	1970	1980	1990	2000	2003	2004	2005
Thousands of tonnes of NO$_2$ from cars	765	989	1324	818	636	597	549

  Catalytic converters were first introduced into Europe in 1985. Legislation requiring them to be fitted to vehicles was introduced in 1993. Use this information, and your own knowledge, to suggest reasons for the changes in NO$_2$ emissions shown in the table.

  _____

  _____

  _____

  _____

  [4 marks]

Pollution indicators

1 The table shows some freshwater animals and the level of oxygen that they need to live.

Animal	Oxygen level needed
Mayfly larva	High
Cased caddis fly larva	Fairly high
Snail	Fairly low
Blood worm	Low
Rat-tailed maggot	Very low

a Explain how a scientist could use this information to quickly find out how much oxygen there is in a river.

_____

_____ [2 marks]

b A stream has raw sewage flowing into it. Which animal would you be most likely to find in the water in the stream? Explain your answer.

_____ [2 marks]

c i Blood worms get their name because they contain the red pigment haemoglobin. Suggest how this helps them to live in their environment.

_____ [2 marks]

ii Blood worms are able to live in conditions where there is plenty of oxygen, but they are not normally found in these areas. Suggest a reason for this.

_____ [2 marks]

Deforestation

2 Some parts of the rainforest in Sarawak have been cut down so that the wood can be sold. The table shows the numbers of some species of animals that lived in an area before the forest was logged, immediately after logging and two years after logging. After logging, the forest slowly regenerated.

Mammal	Mean number of animals per km²		
	Before	Immediately after logging	Two years after logging
Marbled cat	Present	0	0
Oriental small-clawed otter	Present	0	0
Giant squirrel	5.18	1.48	3.75
Smaller species of squirrel	15.82	24.08	103.50
Tree shrews	10.28	4.92	10.04
Barking deer	2.91	0.79	10.22

a Which animals have been worst affected by the logging? Explain your answer.

_____

_____ [2 marks]

b Suggest reasons for the results for tree shrews and barking deer.

_____

_____ [2 marks]

c Suggest reasons for the results for smaller species of squirrel.

_____

_____ [2 marks]

d Apart from the loss of animal species, give **two** other reasons why we should try to reduce the amount of logging of rainforests.

1_____

2_____ [2 marks]

The greenhouse effect – good or bad?

1 The graphs show the changes in average world temperature and carbon dioxide concentration in the air between 1700 and 2000.

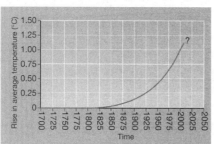 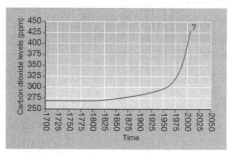

a What can we definitely conclude from these graphs?

A Both carbon dioxide and temperature have increased since 1700.

B Increasing carbon dioxide causes an increase in temperature.

C Increasing temperature causes an increase in carbon dioxide.

D By 2050, the average temperature will be about 1.5 °C higher than in 1700. [1 mark]

b Suggest reasons for the especially rapid increase in carbon dioxide concentration since 1950.

_____

_____

[2 marks]

Sustainability – the way forward?

2 a Jack likes to cycle to school rather than being taken in the car by his father.
He says it keeps him fit and it is a small contribution towards sustainable development.
i Explain what is meant by **sustainable development**.

_____

_____

[2 marks]

ii Suggest how Jack's decision about his journey to school makes a small contribution to sustainable development.

_____

_____

[2 marks]

b The table shows the U-values for different structures in buildings.

Structure	U-values
Tiled roof without insulation	2.0
Tiled roof with insulation	0.3
Cavity wall without insulation	1.4
Cavity wall with foam insulation	0.4
Single-glazed window	5.7
Double-glazed window	2.9

The U-value can be used to calculate the heat energy lost from that part of the building, using the formula:

heat energy loss (watts) = U-value × area (m²) × temperature difference between inside and outside

A house has a tiled roof with no insulation. The family who live in the house like to keep the temperature at 15 °C. Calculate by how much they could reduce the rate of heat loss when the temperature outside is 5 °C, if they insulated their roof.

_____

_____

[2 marks]

B1b revision checklist

I know:

what determines where particular species live

☐ animals and plants are adapted to live in different habitats, to compete for resources and to survive attack from predators

☐ they may have adapted (e.g. thorns, poisons, warning colours) to cope with specific features of their extreme environment

why individuals of the same species are different from each other; and what new methods there are for producing plants and animals with desirable characteristics

☐ DNA is the genetic material that controls inherited characteristics

☐ reproduction can be sexual (genetic variation in offspring) or asexual (identical offspring)

☐ cloning and genetic engineering can be used to produce plants and animals with desirable characteristics

☐ concerns about GM organisms include: their safety for use, genes jumping to other species, and long-term consequences of eating them

☐ cross-species embryo transplantation may help to preserve endangered wild species

why some species of plants and animals have died out and how new species of plants and animals develop

☐ theories of evolution have changed over time; Darwin proposed the theory of evolution by natural selection

☐ fossils tell us how present-day species have evolved and how they compare to prehistoric species

☐ life on Earth may have originated: as a result of early light/air/water conditions; from a meteorite; or in deep oceans

☐ species can become extinct due to environmental change and human impact

how humans affect the environment

☐ increases in human population use up more resources and produce more waste and pollution

☐ human action contributes to acid rain, air pollution, water pollution, over-use of land and loss of diversity in rainforests

☐ living organisms such as lichens, invertebrates and fish can be used as indicators of pollution

☐ increasing the greenhouse effect can lead to climate change

☐ sustainable development, e.g. using renewable energy resources and recycling can help to safeguard the environment for future generations

Elements and the periodic table

1 This question is about the periodic table.

a Name an atom that is in the same group as sodium but has one more shell of electrons.

_____ [1 mark]

b Name an atom that has a relative atomic mass that is double the relative atomic mass of carbon. _____ [1 mark]

c Which atom contains half as many protons as neon?

_____ [1 mark]

d When scientists first tried to put elements in order, they put them in order of their relative atomic masses. Mendeleev changed the order of tellurium iodine (relative atomic mass 128) and iodine (relative atomic mass 127) so that iodine was in Group 7. Explain why this was a better way to classify iodine.

_____

_____ [2 marks]

Atomic structure 1

2 Bromine is an element in the periodic table.

$^{80}_{35}$ **Br** bromine

a Fill in the gaps to show the numbers of the different types of particles in an atom of bromine.

An atom of bromine contains _____ protons, _____

electrons and _____ neutrons. [3 marks]

b When bromine reacts with other elements, it gains electrons. Gaining electrons does not affect the mass of the bromine atoms. Explain why.

_____ [1 mark]

c i Give the symbol of the element that contains atoms with one more proton than bromine.

_____ [1 mark]

ii Give the symbol of an element that is in the same group as bromine but has fewer protons.

_____ [1 mark]

3 This question is about electronic configurations. The electronic configurations of some atoms are shown here:

2, 8, 2	2	2, 8, 1	2, 8
atom A	**atom B**	**atom C**	**atom D**

a i Which atom is from an element in Group 2? _____ [1 mark]

ii Explain how you can tell.

_____ [1 mark]

b i Which atom is a noble gas? _____ [1 mark]

ii Explain how you can tell.

_____ [1 mark]

c Write the electronic configuration of the element that is directly above atom C in the same group.

_____ [1 mark]

Bonding

1 Match formulae, **A**, **B**, **C** and **D**, with the sentences **1 – 4** in the table.

A NaCl

B N_2

C H_2O

D KNO_3

1	2	3	4

1	This is a compound that contains three different types of atom.
2	This is a molecule with two identical atoms joined together.
3	This compound contains a covalent bond between hydrogen and oxygen atoms.
4	This compound contains chloride ions.

[4 marks]

2 This is a diagram of an oxygen molecule. O══O

Which of the following statements about the bonding in an oxygen molecule is correct?

A Atoms are held in a sea of mobile electrons.

B There are four shared electrons between the oxygen atoms.

C There is a single covalent bond between the oxygen atoms.

D The oxygen atoms are held together by ionic attraction.

[1 mark]

Extraction of limestone

3 A company sells large quantities of limestone.

a Give **two** large-scale uses of limestone.

_____

_____ [2 marks]

b The company wants to open a new quarry. Local people protest against the quarry. This is one of the protesters.

Give **three** reasons why local people might protest against a new limestone quarry.

Say NO to the quarry!

_____

_____

_____

_____

[3 marks]

c Suggest **one** argument that the company could use to persuade people that the quarry would benefit local people.

_____ [1 mark]

Thermal decomposition of limestone

1 a When calcium carbonate is heated it reacts to make a solid compound and a gas. Complete the word and symbol equation for the reaction by filling in the boxes.

calcium carbonate → [   ] + [   ]

$CaCO_3$ → CaO + [   ]   [3 marks]

b Eve does an experiment. She weighs a lump of limestone before and after heating it. She finds that the lump is lighter after heating. Which sentence gives the best explanation for this?

A The atoms get smaller when they are heated.

B A gas is given off.

C The limestone has been burned.

D The lump got wet when it was heated.   [1 mark]

---

2 The equation shows what happens when carbon dioxide is bubbled through a solution of calcium hydroxide (limewater).

$CO_2(g)$ + $Ca(OH)_2(aq)$ → $CaCO_3(s)$ + _____

a Complete the equation by filling in the missing formula.   [1 mark]

b Explain why limewater goes cloudy when carbon dioxide is bubbled through it.

_____

_____   [2 marks]

Uses of limestone

3 Cement and concrete are both made using limestone.

a Describe **one** difference between cement and concrete.

_____   [1 mark]

b Cement is used to hold bricks together; concrete is used for making structures such as bridges. Explain why the two materials have different uses.

_____

_____   [2 marks]

---

4 How is toughened glass made?

A By adding metal atoms to the glass when it is made.

B By heating the molten glass to a higher temperature.

C By cooling the molten glass more quickly.

D By using less limestone in the glass mixture.   [1 mark]

D–C

B–A*

D–C

B–A*

The blast furnace

1 Complete the sentences by choosing the **correct** words from the box.

| carbon monoxide | silicon dioxide | oxidation | oxygen | reduction |

In the blast furnace, iron oxide reacts to form iron by reacting with _____.

During the reaction, the iron oxide loses _____.

This type of reaction is called _____.   [3 marks]

2 In the blast furnace, carbon from coke reacts with carbon dioxide to form carbon monoxide.

$$C + CO_2 \rightarrow 2CO$$

What is happening in this reaction?

A thermal decomposition

B oxidation only

C combustion

D both oxidation and reduction   [1 mark]

Using iron

3 The diagrams show the arrangement of atoms in some different materials.

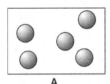 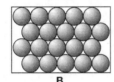 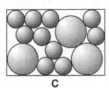

A   B   C

a **i** Which diagram shows the arrangement of atoms in steel?

_____   [1 mark]

ii Explain your reasoning.

_____

_____   [2 marks]

b Why is wrought iron easily shaped?

A The atoms are in layers that can slide over each other.

B The bonds between atoms are weak.

C The atoms are free to move around freely.

D The atoms are far apart from each other.   [1 mark]

Using steel

1 The diagrams show how the atoms are arranged in wrought iron and stainless steel.

wrought iron

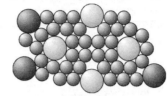

stainless steel

a Describe the difference in the **structure** of wrought iron and stainless steel.

_____

_____

_____ [3 marks]

b Explain why stainless steel is more suitable than wrought iron for making cutlery.

_____

_____ [2 marks]

D–C

Transition metals

2 The diagram shows the structure of a metal.

a Name the **two** types of particles shown in the diagram.

_____ and _____ [2 marks]

b Use the diagram to explain why metals conduct electricity.

_____

_____ [2 marks]

D–C

3 The table shows some information about some metals.

B–A*

Metal	Transition element?	Radius of one atom (nm)	Melting point (°C)	Strength of metal
Sodium	No	0.2	98	Very weak
Iron	Yes	0.1	1535	High
Calcium	No	0.2	850	Weak
Cobalt	Yes	0.1	1492	High

a Which **two** metals in the table are transition metals?

_____ and _____ [2 marks]

b How do the properties of transition metals differ from the other metals in the table?

A They have higher melting points but are weaker.

B They have smaller atoms and lower melting points.

C They have smaller atoms and are weaker.

D They have higher melting points and are stronger. [1 mark]

Aluminium

D–C

1 a Aluminium is extracted from aluminium oxide using electrolysis.
Complete the sentences about electrolysis.

Aluminium cannot be extracted by reacting with carbon because it is too _____.

During electrolysis the positive aluminium ions are attracted to the _____ electrode.

The ions form aluminium atoms when they _____ electrons. [3 marks]

B–A*

b During electrolysis, oxygen ions gain electrons to form oxygen.

i Balance the equation.

$$2O^{2-} \rightarrow \underline{\hspace{2cm}} e^- + O_2$$ [1 mark]

ii Does this reaction involve oxidation or reduction? Explain your reasoning.

_____

_____ [2 marks]

B–A*

2 In the process of electrolysis of aluminium, cryolite is added. Why does adding cryolite lower the cost of the process?

A cryolite acts as a cheap fuel

B adding cryolite means less aluminium oxide needs to be used

C cryolite reduces aluminium ions

D molten cryolite acts as a solvent for aluminium oxide [1 mark]

Aluminium recycling

D–C

3 Here is some information about aluminium.

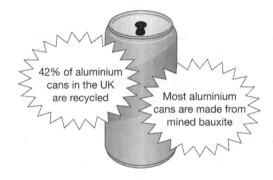

42% of aluminium cans in the UK are recycled

Most aluminium cans are made from mined bauxite

a Bauxite is the main ore that is used to make aluminium. Give **two disadvantages** of mining bauxite.

_____

_____ [2 marks]

b Suggest reasons why **less than half** the aluminium cans we use are recycled.

_____

_____ [2 marks]

Titanium

1 The table shows some information about titanium, aluminium and iron.

	Titanium	Aluminium	Iron
Density in g/cm³	4.5	2.7	7.9
Melting point °C	1675	660	1535
Corrosion resistance	Does not corrode	Does not corrode	Corrodes
Main oxide in ore	TiO_2	Al_2O_3	Fe_2O_3
Bonding in oxide	Covalent	Ionic	Ionic
Cost of extraction	Very high	High	Low

a Titanium and aluminium are used to make bicycle frames. Use information from the table to explain why they are better metals to use than iron.

_____

_____

_____ [3 marks]

b i Aluminium is extracted by electrolysis of molten aluminium oxide.
Use information from the table to explain why molten aluminium oxide conducts electricity but molten titanium oxide does not.

_____

_____ [2 marks]

ii Aluminium is electrolysed at 900 °C. At this temperature, the aluminium leaves the electrolysis tank as a liquid.
Explain why titanium is not a liquid at this temperature.

_____ [1 mark]

Copper

2 The supplies of high quality copper ores are running out.

a Why does extracting copper from very low grade ores cause more environmental damage?

A The ores must be crushed and washed.

B Very large volumes of rock must be extracted to produce a small amount of copper.

C Copper ions are toxic to most living things.

D Copper ores produce sulfur dioxide when they are heated. [1 mark]

b Copper can be extracted from old mine waste heaps by leaching. What does the term **leaching** mean?

A Electrolysing a dilute solution of copper.

B Crushing the waste ore to increase its surface area.

C Dissolving copper ores in dilute acid.

D Roasting the waste ore in air. [1 mark]

3 Bronze is used to make coins. Which of the following statements about bronze is true?

A Bronze is an alloy of non-metals.

B Bronze is a transition metal element.

C Bronze contains a mixture of copper and tin.

D Bronze is a compound of copper and zinc. [1 mark]

Smart alloys

1 One use of smart alloys is for making braces to straighten teeth.
The diagram shows some information about smart alloys.

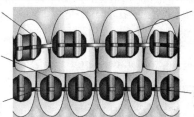

This smart alloy is made from nickel and titanium

Smart alloys are mixtures of different elements

Smart alloys have a 'shape' memory

Smart alloys can be bent and stretched into different shapes

Smart alloys contain mainly metal atoms

a Complete the sentences about smart alloys.
Smart alloys are **similar** to normal alloys because _____

_____

_____

Smart alloys are **different** from normal alloys because _____

_____

_____ [4 marks]

b What do you have to do to a smart alloy to return it to its original shape?

_____

_____ [2 marks]

Fuels of the future

2 Car exhaust emissions release pollutant gases into the atmosphere.

a Which exhaust gases are a result of incomplete combustion in the car engine?

A sulfur dioxide and carbon dioxide

B nitrogen and carbon dioxide

C petrol vapour and carbon monoxide

D nitrogen dioxide and sulfur dioxide

b Which of the following gases is **not** produced by reactions in a catalytic converter?

A carbon dioxide

B water vapour

C nitrogen

D hydrogen

3 Claudia and Saul are discussing whether electric trams cause less pollution than buses.

a Explain why using electric trams gives out less pollution than buses in the city.

The trams give out much less pollution than buses – they are a real benefit to the environment.

I'm not so sure – surely using electricity must be harmful to the environment?

_____

_____

_____ [2 marks]

b Why is using electricity harmful to the environment?

_____

_____ [2 marks]

Crude oil

1 Crude oil is separated by fractional distillation.

a Match descriptions, **A**, **B**, **C** and **D**, to the numbers **1 – 4** on the diagram.

A the oil evaporates here

B condensation happens here

C this is the coolest part of the column

D molecules with the highest boiling point leave the column here

1	2	3	4

[4 marks]

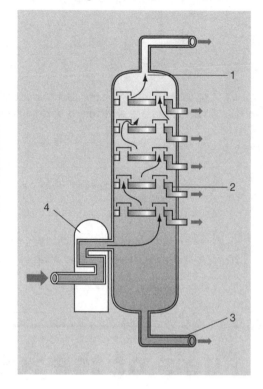

D–C

b Which fraction leaving the column has the strongest intermolecular forces between its molecules?

A the fraction leaving the top of the column

B the fraction containing the largest molecules

C the fraction with the lowest boiling point

D the fraction containing the lowest number of carbon atoms

[1 mark]

B–A*

Alkanes

2 The diagrams show the structures of some alkane molecules.

B–A*

```
                          H
                          |
   H H H H H           H-C-H             H H H          H H H H
   | | | | |           H | H             | | |          | | | |
H-C-C-C-C-C-H       H-C-C-C-H         H-C-C-C-H      H-C-C-C-C-H
   | | | | |           | | |             | | |          | | | |
   H H H H H           H H H             H H H          H H H H

      A                   B                 C              D
```

a Which alkane has the highest boiling point? _____ [1 mark]

b Which **two** alkanes are isomers of each other? _____ [1 mark]

c Which alkane **cannot** form isomers? _____ [1 mark]

d Which alkane is called propane? _____ [1 mark]

B–A*

D–C

Pollution problems

1 Petrol mainly contains hydrocarbons but also contains small amounts of sulfur as an impurity.

a Complete the equations to show what happens when petrol burns completely.

hydrocarbon + _____ → _____ + _____

sulfur + _____ → _____ [4 marks]

b Burning petrol adds to the acid rain problem. Fish caught in lakes affected by acid rain are usually older and larger. Explain why fewer young, small fish are found.

_____

_____ [2 marks]

2 An article about pollution from burning petrol contains this information.

PETROL TO PUT US IN THE DARK?
We need to find ways to use less petrol. Don't forget that petrol is a non-renewable fuel. Apart from all the well-known environmental problems from burning petrol, it might also lead to global dimming – a worrying thought!

a What does the article mean when it says that petrol is **non-renewable**?
  A Burning petrol gives off carbon dioxide that may cause climate change.
  B We use huge quantities of petrol worldwide.
  C Supplies of petrol cannot be replaced when they are used.
  D Not all pollution from petrol can be removed by a catalytic converter. [1 mark]

b Which of the following is a correct explanation of **global dimming**?
  A Water from melting ice caps cause clouds that cut out sunlight.
  B Pollution reduces the light that can pass through the ozone layer.
  C Particles of carbon from burning fuels block out the sunlight.
  D Increased carbon dioxide absorbs energy from the Sun.

_____ and _____ [2 marks]

Reducing sulfur problems

3 All petrol garages in the United Kingdom sell low sulfur petrol.

Which of these statements about sulfur in petrol are true?

A Petrol companies used to mix sulfur compounds into petrol.

B Sulfur is now removed from petrol using a solvent.

C Sulfur in petrol harms the ozone layer.

D Sulfur in petrol is oxidised when the petrol burns.

_____ and _____ [2 marks]

000.00
000.00

ULTRA LOW
SULFUR PETROL

4 Many scientists think that using aeroplanes is very damaging to the environment because each journey burns very large amounts of fuel and produces large amounts of pollutant gases. Some people who are very concerned about the environment choose to go on holiday by ship.

a Why does burning large amounts of fuel lead to environmental damage?

_____

_____ [2 marks]

b Explain how environmental damage can also be caused by ship travel.

_____

_____ [2 marks]

C1a revision checklist

I know:

how rocks provide building materials

☐ limestone, calcium carbonate, can be used to make cement, mortar, concrete and glass which are used as building materials

☐ an element consists of one type of atom; two atoms of the same element can join together to form a molecule; a compound consists of atoms of two or more elements joined together

☐ atoms are held together in molecules and lattices by chemical bonds, which involves giving, taking or sharing electrons

☐ the electronic configuration of an atom shows the number of its electrons and their arrangement in shells; atoms with a full outermost shell of electrons are stable

☐ how to interpret chemical equations in symbol form and balance equations in terms of numbers of atoms

how rocks provide metals and how metals are used

☐ metals are extracted from their ores, often oxides, by reduction with carbon (iron), electrolysis (aluminium and copper) or other chemical reactions (titanium)

☐ pure metals are soft and easily shaped because the atoms form a regular arrangement – the layers of atoms can slide easily over each other

☐ metals are mixed together to make alloys (e.g. iron and other metals or carbon make steel)

☐ aluminium is expensive to produce, is often too soft on its own, but forms strong alloys with other metals

☐ copper is a hard, strong, good conductor and can be used for wiring and plumbing

☐ aluminium and titanium are resistant to corrosion and have a low density

how we get fuels from crude oil

☐ crude oil is a mixture of hydrocarbon compounds that can be separated by fractional distillation; some fractions can be used as fuels

☐ most of the compounds in crude oil are saturated hydrocarbons called alkanes, which have the general formula C_nH_{2n+2}

☐ burning fossil fuels releases useful energy but also harmful substances, e.g. sulfur dioxide causes acid rain; carbon dioxide causes climate change; smoke particles cause global dimming

Cracking

D–C

1 This molecule is made in a cracking reaction.

Which of the following statements is **not** true for this molecule?

A It is called propene.

B It is a hydrocarbon.

C It is a saturated molecule.

D It contains some single bonds. [1 mark]

B–A*

2 Which of the following molecules **cannot** be made by cracking decane $C_{10}H_{22}$?

A C_2H_4 **B** C_3H_8 **C** C_3H_{10} **D** $C_{12}H_{24}$ [1 mark]

B–A*

3 Novane, C_9H_{20}, is an alkane. Novane can be cracked to form hexane and one other molecule, molecule A.

a i Draw the structure of molecule A in the box. [1 mark]

    ii What is the name of molecule A?

_____ [1 mark]

Alkenes

D–C

4 When alkanes in crude oil are cracked some alkenes are formed.

a Butene is an alkene. It has the formula C_4H_8. Pentene has one more carbon atom than butene. What is the formula for pentene?

_____ [1 mark]

B–A*

b Which of the following statements is true for alkenes?

    A contain only single bonds

    B are saturated

    C contain the same number of hydrogen atoms as carbon atoms

    D have the general formula $C_nH_{(2n+2)}$ [1 mark]

B–A*

5 Ethene gas is used by suppliers of very large supermarkets to make fruit ready for sale.

a Explain why fruit can be made ready for sale by being treated with ethene gas.

_____ [1 mark]

b Explain why fresh flowers are kept **away** from ethene gas.

_____ [1 mark]

Making ethanol

1 This information appeared in a newspaper article about ethanol.

BIOFUELS FOR THE FUTURE
Fuels such as petrol and diesel could soon be replaced by renewable biofuels that contain ethanol made from sugar beet. These new biofuels could solve our problems of relying on finite crude oil reserves.

Many farmers already use biofuels for farm vehicles.

a Explain how sugar beet can be used to produce ethanol.

_____

_____ [2 marks]

b Explain why ethanol made in this way is a 'renewable biofuel'.

_____

_____ [3 marks]

c Ethanol, C_2H_5OH, can also be made by passing a mixture of ethene and steam over a catalyst.

i Write a symbol equation for the reaction.

_____ [2 marks]

ii Explain why ethanol is **not** a hydrocarbon.

_____ [1 mark]

D–C

B–A*

Plastics from alkenes

2 The diagrams show two compounds that contain fluorine.

$$\begin{array}{c} F \\ | \\ F \end{array} C = C \begin{array}{c} F \\ | \\ F \end{array}$$

$$H - \overset{F}{\underset{F}{C}} - \overset{F}{\underset{F}{C}} - H$$

compound A   compound B

a Compound A forms a polymer. Draw a diagram to show the structure of the polymer that forms from compound A.

[2 marks]

b Explain why compound B cannot form a polymer.

_____ [1 mark]

B–A*

3 Which of the following is most likely to be made from a **smart polymer**?

A plastic lenses for spectacles that darken in bright light

B metal electrical wiring in a computer

C plastic food containers that can be thrown away

D metal car bumpers that can be beaten back to shape after accidents [1 mark]

B–A*

Polymers are useful

1 Look at the structures of polymers **A**, **B**, **C** and **D**.

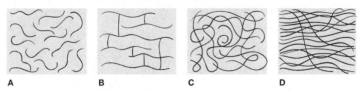

A   B   C   D

a Which polymer contains **cross links**?

_____ [1 mark]

b Which polymer has the highest **density**?

_____ [1 mark]

c Polymers A and C are heated until they go soft and runny. Explain why polymer A is softer and runnier than polymer C.

_____

_____ [2 marks]

2 Which one of the following statements is true for shape memory polymers?

A All shape memory polymers are biodegradable.

B An irreversible change happens when shape memory polymers are heated.

C At higher temperatures the structure of shape memory polymers returns to its original state.

D Shape memory polymers are elastic materials that bounce back to their original shape. [1 mark]

Disposing of polymers

3 The table shows some methods of disposing of waste plastics.

Method of disposal	How it is carried out	Advantage
Burning	Waste is burned in an incinerator	Energy can be used to make electricity
Landfill	Waste is buried in the ground	No need to sort the waste, very cheap
Recycling	Waste is processed to make new polymers	New polymers can be used to make new products such as coat padding
Making biodegradable polymers	Polymers are designed to rot away after being used	Waste is not a long term problem

Which **two** methods reduce the need to use fossil fuels? Explain your reasoning.

1 _____

_____

2 _____

_____ [2 marks]

4 Pins made from both metals and polymers can be used to hold two broken leg bones together while they heal. The patient's leg is cut open and the pins are put through the bone. Explain why polymers are more suitable than metals for use inside the body.

_____

_____ [2 marks]

Oil from plants

1 Vegetable oil made from crushed seeds contains a lot of impurities. The diagram shows an apparatus that can be used to separate pure oil from the mixture.

a Label the diagram by filling in the empty boxes.

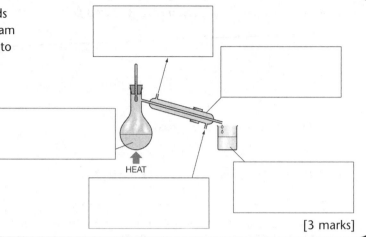

HEAT

[3 marks]

D–C

2 Why are omega-3 fatty acids beneficial to people's health?

A Walnuts are very high in omega-3 fatty acids.

B Omega-3 fatty acids are lower in fat than other fatty acids.

C Omega-3 fatty acids raise blood pressure.

D Omega-3 fatty acids reduce levels of fat in the blood.

[1 mark]

B–A*

Green energy

3 Harriet is not sure that biofuels are a good idea. This is what she has to say.

Growing plants for biofuels uses up a lot of land that we need to grow food. Some oils that come from plants are far too thick to be used for most engines. They cost a lot more to produce than petrol.

a Harriet says that some oils are too thick to be used in engines. How is this problem overcome?

_____ [1 mark]

b Harriet talks about the disadvantages of using biofuels. Give **two advantages** of using biofuels.

_____
_____ [2 marks]

c In the future, petrol will become more expensive than biofuels. Explain why.

_____
_____ [2 marks]

d Biodiesel is one type of biofuel. Biodiesel is a renewable fuel. Give **two** other advantages of using biodiesel rather than standard diesel as a fuel.

_____
_____ [2 marks]

D–C

B–A*

Emulsions

D–C

1 The diagrams show what some different types of emulsions contain.

a Complete the table about these emulsions. Use the words in the box.

Shaving foam contains air bubbles spread out in a liquid.

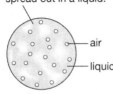

— air

— liquid

shaving foam

After shave cream has water droplets spread out in an oil.

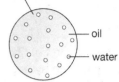

— oil

— water

after shave cream

air	oil	liquid	water

Type of emulsion	Dispersed phase	Continuous phase
Shaving foam		
After shave cream		

[2 marks]

b The ingredients in these emulsions are immiscible. What does **immiscible** mean?

_____

[1 mark]

B–A*

2 Which of the following statements about mayonnaise is true?

A Egg yolk in mayonnaise makes the ingredients immiscible.

B Oil and water in mayonnaise forms layers because they are miscible.

C The continuous phase in mayonnaise is water.

D Vinegar is used in mayonnaise as an oil.

[1 mark]

Polyunsaturates

D–C

3 Olive oil is a **monounsaturated oil**. It contains one double bond.

a How is the bonding in a **saturated fat** different from olive oil?

_____

[1 mark]

b How is the bonding in a **polyunsaturated oil** different from olive oil?

_____

[1 mark]

c Complete the table to show the observations you would expect when each oil or fat reacts with **bromine water**.

Type	Olive oil	Saturated fat	Polyunsaturated oil
Observations	Orange to colourless		

[2 marks]

B–A*

4 Tim's doctor tells him that he has high blood cholesterol levels. The doctor advises Tim

A to eat fats from vegetable oils rather than animal fats.

B to eat more saturated fat to lower cholesterol.

C that monounsaturated fats are better at lowering cholesterol than polyunsaturated fats.

D that high cholesterol is worrying because it widens the arteries.

[1 mark]

Making margarine

---

1 The diagram in box 1 shows part of a molecule of vegetable oil.

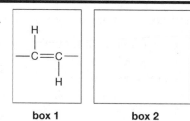

box 1   box 2

a Draw a similar diagram in box 2 to show the same molecule after it has been hydrogenated.

[2 marks]

b Give **two** ways hat his process can be speeded up when it is carried out on an industrial scale.

_____

_____

[2 marks]

---

2 Match words, **A**, **B**, **C** and **D**, with the sentences **1 – 4** in the table.

A HDL cholesterol

B LDL cholesterol

C hydrogenated vegetable oil

D trans free fat

1	2	3	4

1	this can be used to make softer margarines
2	eating this can lead to increased blood pressure
3	this compound in the blood is linked to high blood pressure
4	eating trans fats reduces the concentration of this compound in the blood

[4 marks]

Food additives

---

3 The table shows some information about food additives with E-numbers.

Purpose	Number
Colouring	E100-181
Preservative	E200-285 and 1105
Antioxidant	E300-340
Emulsifier	E400-499

a A cake contains the additive E220 and E340. Explain why manufacturers add these additives to foods such as cake.

_____

_____

_____

[3 marks]

b The manufacturers used to use additive E102. This additive has since been banned. Explain why it is sometimes necessary to ban food additives.

_____

_____

[2 marks]

Analysing chemicals

1 One method of testing dyes used in foods is by using chromatography. This chromatogram shows four known food dyes, **A**, **B**, **C** and **D** and an unknown dye used to colour sweets.

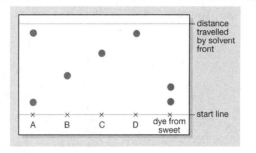

a Food dye **A** is banned because one of its ingredients is harmful. Food dye **D** is not banned. Does the sweet contain the harmful ingredient? Explain your reasoning.

_____

_____

_____

[3 marks]

b Ruby wants to calculate the retention factor of dye **B**. Write a set of instructions to tell her how to do this.

_____

_____

_____

[3 marks]

c Dye **C** has a retention factor of 0.75. The solvent front is 4 cm above the start line. How far above the start line did the spot from dye **C** travel?

_____

_____

_____

[3 marks]

The Earth

2 The diagram shows the structure of the Earth.

Match words, **A**, **B**, **C** and **D**, to the sentences **1 – 4** in the table.

A mantle

B inner core

C outer core

D crust

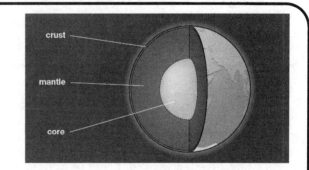

1	this is the furthest from the Earth's surface
2	a thin layer of solid rock
3	convection currents here reshape the Earth's surface
4	this contains a liquid mixture of iron and nickel

1	2	3	4

[4 marks]

3 The magnetic field of the Earth

A has a particular strength that remains constant.

B protects us from harmful UV light from the Sun.

C repels electrically charged particles.

D creates an effect called the solar wind.

[1 mark]

Earth's surface

1 a The diagram shows the continent of Pangaea 200 million years ago.

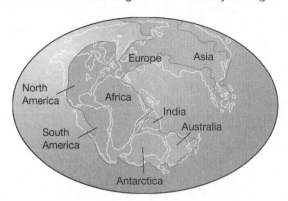

The sentences describe how the continents moved to their current positions.
Match words, **A**, **B**, **C** and **D**, to the numbers **1 – 4** in the sentences.

A lithosphere **B** convection currents **C** tectonic plates **D** mantle

The upper mantle and crust form the Earth's _____ **1** _____ .

The continents are carried on large masses of rock called _____ **2** _____ .

Heat from the Earth's core causes the rocks to move by _____ **3** _____ .

This happens in the _____ **4** _____ .

1	2	3	4

[4 marks]

b Europe and North America were joined 200 million years ago. Nowadays,
they are separated by the vast ocean of the Atlantic. This change happened because

A new rock formed at a mid-ocean ridge.

B magma rose to the surface near a subduction zone.

C a continental plate rose over an oceanic plate.

D earthquakes caused a sudden movement of rock.

[1 mark]

Earthquakes and volcanoes

2 a Look at the diagram that shows where two plates meet.
Match sentences, **A**, **B**, **C** and **D**, with the numbers **1 – 4**
on the diagram.

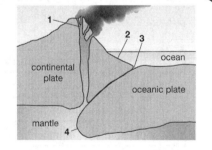

A earthquakes are most likely to happen here

B rock is melting here

C rock is being pushed up here

1	2	3	4

D lava is cooling down most
quickly here

[4 marks]

b Which of the plates, the continental plate or the oceanic plate is the **least** dense?
Explain your reasoning.

_____

[1 mark]

c Explain why this diagram shows an example of a subduction zone.

_____

_____

[1 mark]

The air

1 The gases in the atmosphere

A are all pure elements.

B are all pure compounds.

C contain molecules that are a mixture of metals and non-metals.

D contain a mixture of molecules of non-metals. [1 mark]

2 Airbags work because the crash triggers the following reaction.

$$2NaN_3 \rightarrow \underline{\hspace{2cm}} N_2 + \underline{\hspace{2cm}} Na$$

a Balance the equation. [1 mark]

b Give the names of the products of the reaction.

_____ [1 mark]

c Explain why this reaction causes the airbag to inflate.

_____ [2 marks]

Evolution of the air

3 This table shows gases coming from a modern active volcano on a Pacific island. The **temperature** of the volcano is over **1000 °C**.

Name of gas	Percentage of gas
Water	37.1
Carbon dioxide	48.9
Sulfur dioxide	11.8
Hydrogen	0.49
Carbon monoxide	1.51

a **i** Why is water a gas when it comes out of the volcano?

_____ [1 mark]

ii The Earth's early atmosphere contained large amounts of water vapour. Describe what happened to all this water vapour.

_____

_____ [3 marks]

b Scientists think that our early atmosphere came from volcanoes.
i Which gas is present in the **largest quantity** in the gases from this volcano?

_____ [1 mark]

ii What **two** processes removed most of this gas from the early atmosphere?

_____ [2 marks]

c Give **two** other important differences between the gases from this volcano and our modern atmosphere.

_____

_____ [2 marks]

4 The Earth and the Moon are both the same distance from the Sun. The Earth has an average surface temperature of 17 °C. The average surface temperature of the moon is – 33°C. Use ideas about the atmosphere to explain why the surface temperatures are so different.

_____

_____ [3 marks]

Atmospheric change

1 Some friends are discussing the environment. This is what they have to say.

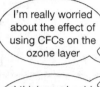

I'm really worried about the effect of using CFCs on the ozone layer

I think we should plant more trees in forests

I think we should all burn biofuels

I think it is ridiculous the amount of fossil fuels we burn

Put ticks (✓) in the table to show whether each activity increases, decreases or makes no difference to the amount of carbon dioxide in the air.

Activity	Decreases amount of carbon dioxide in air	Increases amount of carbon dioxide in air	Does not affect amount of carbon dioxide in air
Using CFCs			
Planting more trees			
Burning biofuels			
Burning fossil fuels			

[4 marks]

2 The Earth stores carbon dioxide in carbon sinks. Plants are one type of carbon sink.

a Choose the names of two other types of carbon sinks. Draw a ring around **two correct** answers.

crude oil   **rainwater**   **limestone**   **photosynthesis**   **respiration**   [2 marks]

b Plants act as carbon sinks. Trees are much better carbon sinks than short-lived plants, such as grass. Explain why.

_____

_____   [2 marks]

c The seas contains large amounts of dissolved carbon dioxide. More carbon dioxide can dissolve in cold water than in warm water. Scientists are worried that if the climate gets warmer, the amount of carbon dioxide in the **air** will increase very quickly. Explain how this could happen.

_____

_____   [2 marks]

3 Most people think that the average surface temperature of Earth is increasing due to increased concentrations of carbon dioxide in the atmosphere. Some scientists do not agree. They think that the increase in temperature is due to changes in the Sun's activity. Which statement supports the scientists' views?

A Different planets in the solar system have different surface temperatures.

B Not all planets in the solar system have an atmosphere.

C The surface temperature of other planets in our Solar System has risen over the last 100 years.

D Not all planet atmospheres contain carbon dioxide.   [1 mark]

C1b revision checklist

I know:

how polymers and ethanol are made from oil

☐ crude oil is made from long-chain hydrocarbons that can be cracked by thermal decomposition to form shorter-chain alkanes and alkenes

☐ alkenes are unsaturated hydrocarbons, they contain double carbon-carbon bonds and have the general formula C_nH_{2n}

☐ alkenes can be made into polymers, which are long-chain molecules created when lots of small molecules called monomers are joined together in polymerisation

☐ polymers can be used to make useful substances, e.g. waterproof materials and plastics, but many are not biodegradable

how plant oils can be used

☐ vegetable oils can be hardened to make margarine in a process called hydrogenation

☐ biodiesel fuel can be produced from vegetable oils

☐ oils do not dissolve in water; they can be used to produce emulsions, e.g. in salad dressings

☐ processed foods may contain additives to improve appearance, taste and shelf-life; E-numbers identify permitted additives and must be listed; some additives can be harmful and may be banned

☐ chemical analysis can be used to identify additives and food colouring in foods, e.g. by paper chromatography

what the changes are in the Earth and its atmosphere

☐ the Earth has three main layers: the crust, mantle and core

☐ the Earth's atmosphere has changed over millions of years; many of the gases that make up the atmosphere came from volcanoes

☐ for 200 million years, the proportions of different gases in the atmosphere have been much the same as they are today

☐ human activities have recently produced further changes, e.g. the levels of greenhouse gases are rising

Heat energy

1 Thermal radiation is a type of **electromagnetic** wave.

a Write down **three** properties of thermal radiation.

_____

_____ [3 marks]

b Emily has just moved to a new house which has large south-facing windows. During the summer the house gets very hot.
i Explain why the house stays cooler if she draws the curtains in the daytime.

_____

_____ [2 marks]

ii Her friend suggests that she could paint the outside of her house a different colour. Explain how this would help the house feel cooler in summer.

_____

_____ [3 marks]

D–C

2 Craig has made some biscuits.

a Explain why the uncooked biscuits have less internal energy compared with the biscuits when they are cooking in the oven.

_____ [1 mark]

b Write down how temperature and internal energy are connected.

_____

_____ [2 marks]

B–A*

Thermal radiation

3 Match words, **A**, **B**, **C** and **D**, with the numbers **1 – 4** in the sentences.

A reduce   **B** absorb   **C** reflect   **D** increase

White surfaces ____ **1** ____ heat well and ____ **2** ____ heat badly.

One company painted the outside of its refrigerated lorries white

to ____ **3** ____ heat transfers and keep the food cool. Painting the

lorry black would ____ **4** ____ heat transfers.

1	2	3	4

[4 marks]

D–C

4 a Write down **two** factors that affect the amount of thermal energy an object has.

_____

_____ [2 marks]

b Explain why an ice cube has less thermal energy than the drink it is in.

_____

_____ [2 marks]

c Explain why a thermal imaging camera will detect the drink more easily before the ice cube is added.

_____

_____ [2 marks]

B–A*

Conduction and convection

1 One end of a metal rod is placed in the flame of a Bunsen burner. After a while, the other end of the rod becomes hot.

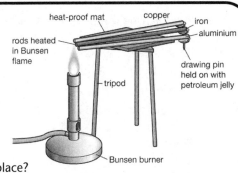

heat-proof mat   copper
iron
aluminium
rods heated in Bunsen flame
drawing pin held on with petroleum jelly
tripod
Bunsen burner

a What is the name of the type of heat transfer that takes place?

_____   [1 mark]

b Explain how heat is transferred from one end of the metal rod to the other.

_____

_____

_____   [3 marks]

c The experiment is repeated with a metal rod and a glass rod. Explain why the glass rod does not conduct the heat as well as the metal rod.

_____

_____   [2 marks]

2 Match words, **A**, **B**, **C** and **D**, with the numbers **1 – 4** in the sentences.

A heat capacity   **B** temperature   **C** thermal energy   **D** warm

A hot water bottle stores more ____ **1** ____ than a bottle of hot

air at the same ____ **2** ____. The water has a higher ____ **3** ____,

and stays ____ **4** ____ for longer.

1	2	3	4

[4 marks]

Heat transfer

3 a A diamond feels very cold to touch. This means that
   A it is a bad heat conductor.
   B it is cooler than its surroundings.
   C it has a low specific heat capacity.
   D it is a good heat conductor.   [1 mark]

b A diamond has no free electrons. It conducts heat because its atoms
   A are very closely linked.
   B are so loosely linked that they can change places.
   C vibrate easily.
   D have a high heat capacity.   [1 mark]

c Convection currents occur in liquids because
   A heated fluids are more dense than cool fluids.
   B heated fluids are less dense than cool fluids.
   C energy is transferred when the atoms vibrate.
   D they have free electrons.   [1 mark]

d The particles in gases are not close together which means that
   A they are poor convectors and good heat conductors.
   B they are poor convectors and poor heat conductors.
   C they are good convectors and poor heat conductors.
   D they are good convectors and good heat conductors.   [1 mark]

D–C

B–A*

B–A*

D–C

Types of energy

1 a A book lying on the top of a wall has _____ energy.
   A chemical
   B potential
   C kinetic
   D sound   [1 mark]

b Energy is measured in
   A joules
   B watts
   C metres
   D kilograms   [1 mark]

c Energy can be stored in these forms
   A light and kinetic
   B kinetic and potential
   C chemical and potential
   D electrical and chemical   [1 mark]

d Fossil fuels were created as a result of
   A global warming.
   B the Sun's radiation over recent years.
   C human activity.
   D the Sun's radiation over millions of years.   [1 mark]

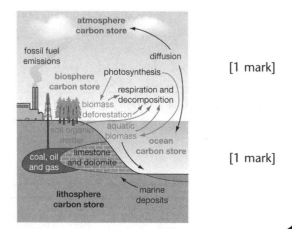

Energy changes

2 George drives his car along a level road.

a Some of the energy is wasted. Write down **two** forms of wasted energy produced by the car.

_____ [2 marks]

b Explain what happens to the wasted energy.

_____

_____ [2 marks]

c Describe how the energy from the fuel is transformed as George drives his car up a hill and then stops it.

_____

_____

_____

_____ [4 marks]

3 Match words, **A**, **B**, **C** and **D**, with the numbers **1 – 4** in the sentences.

A energy   **B** mass   **C** fusion   **D** conservation

1	2	3	4

The law of Energy ____ **1** ____ says that energy cannot be created or destroyed.

In the Sun, energy is given out due to nuclear ____ **2** ____. The ____ **3** ____ of the nuclei

changes into energy directly. In the Sun, both mass and ____ **4** ____ are conserved.   [4 marks]

Energy diagrams

1 The picture shows a Sankey diagram for a petrol engine.

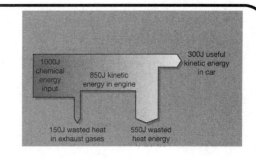

a Complete this equation:

energy input = energy _____ = useful energy

+ _____ energy   [2 marks]

b The energy transformation takes place in two stages in the car. State where most of the energy wastage takes place.

_____

[1 mark]

c An improved engine has been designed. It changes 1000 J of chemical energy into 500 J of kinetic energy. The rest is wasted heat. Draw a Sankey diagram to show this.

[4 marks]

2 Match words, **A**, **B**, **C** and **D**, with the numbers **1 – 4** in the sentences.

A rechargeable   **B** electricity   **C** energy   **D** pollution

An electric car uses a ____ **1** ____ battery. The ____ **2** ____ in the battery comes from power stations. The car does not pollute the roads, but the power stations providing ____ **3** ____ to charge the battery cause ____ **4** ____.

1	2	3	4

[4 marks]

Energy and heat

3 a Wasted energy is transferred to the surroundings, which
A concentrate the energy for future use.
B store the energy.
C heat up.
D cool down.   [1 mark]

b When a plate heats up, its particles
A vibrate more vigorously.
B start vibrating.
C change places.
D spread out.   [1 mark]

c Useful sources of energy are normally
A diluted
B concentrated
C spread out
D hard to find   [1 mark]

d A fridge transfers heat in the opposite direction to normal. A power supply is needed because
A it provides cold energy to the fridge.
B heat energy is needed for the fridge to work properly.
C energy is needed to spread the heat out.
D energy is needed to concentrate and transfer the heat.   [1 mark]

Energy, work and power

1 The weight of Molly and her skis is 500 N. A ski lift carries her to the top of the slope, which is a height of 60 m.

a How much **work** is done by the ski lift?

_____ joules   [3 marks]

b If this took 75 seconds, work out the **power** of the ski lift.

_____ watts   [3 marks]

c The ski lift is replaced by a more **efficient** model. Explain why the energy used by the new ski lift will be less than the energy used by the first lift.

_____

_____   [2 marks]

d Explain why the force needed to lift Molly vertically up a mountain slope would be greater than the force needed to lift her along a slope to the same point.

_____

_____   [2 marks]

Efficiency

2 a Efficiency compares
   A energy usefully transferred with work done.
   B energy usefully transferred with total energy supplied.
   C wasted energy with total energy supplied.
   D percentage of wasted energy with work done.   [1 mark]

b The power of a kettle is 200 kW. The energy used by the kettle in one minute is
   A 12 000 kJ
   B 200 kJ
   C 12 000 kW
   D 200 kW   [1 mark]

c A kettle uses 170 kJ to heat water. 200 kJ of electrical energy is supplied to the kettle. The kettle's efficiency is
   A 118%
   B 60%
   C 85%
   D 8.5%   [1 mark]

d A perpetual motion machine will never work because
   A science is not advanced enough.
   B they use up too much energy.
   C energy cannot be transformed in two directions.
   D some energy is always wasted with any energy transfer. [1 mark]

Using energy effectively

1 Luke is worried that he is wasting energy at home.

a How can he reduce the energy spent on lighting?

_____

_____ [2 marks]

b Why is it a good idea for Luke to install insulation?

_____ [1 mark]

2

Type of insulation	Installation cost (in £)	Annual saving (in £)	Payback time (in years)
Loft insulation	240	60	4
Cavity wall insulation	360	60	6
Draught-proofing doors and windows	45	15	3
Double glazing	2500	25	100

a Explain what is meant by **payback time**.

_____

_____ [2 marks]

b The Brown family are planning to stay in their house for ten years and would like to install some insulation. Use the table to explain why draught proofing is not the best insulation method for them. Include a calculation for full marks.

_____

_____

_____ [3 marks]

c Government grants are available for homeowners to install solar panels, but this may not save energy nationally. Write down **two** disadvantages of installing solar panels.

_____

_____ [2 marks]

Why use electricity?

3 a Mains electricity is very useful because
A it can be stored.
B it is an instant, convenient supply of energy.
C using electricity does not contribute to global warming.
D there are lots of uses for energy in the form of electricity. [1 mark]

b Batteries are useful because
A they are cheap to use.
B they can store larges amounts of energy.
C they are portable and can supply electricity.
D they store electricity. [1 mark]

c When there is no source of electricity
A batteries can be recharged using solar energy or clockwork springs.
B batteries cannot be charged up.
C batteries cannot be used.
D batteries can only be recharged by plugging them into a socket. [1 mark]

d LEDs are being used in torches instead of bulbs. Batteries in these torches last longer because
A LEDs use a larger current than bulbs.
B LEDs use electrons.
C LEDs are different colours.
D LEDs use less energy than bulbs do. [1 mark]

Pascal content

Electricity and heat

1 a Write down **two** factors that affect the resistance of a wire.

_____ [2 marks]

b Explain why a radio uses a thinner flex than an electric cooker.

_____ [1 mark]

c Fuse wires have different ratings. Explain why the cooker needs a higher rated fuse than the radio.

_____ [2 marks]

D–C

2 An MRI scanner uses superconductors.

a How does the resistance of a superconductor change with temperature?

_____ [1 mark]

b Explain why a superconductor has low heat losses due to the currents flowing through it.

_____ [2 marks]

c Write down **one** reason why superconductors are not used often in everyday activities.

_____ [1 mark]

B–A*

The cost of electricity

3

Appliance	Power rating	Appliance	Power rating
Laptop computer	100 W	Television	50 W
Electric kettle	2.4 kW	Microwave oven	1.2 kW
Hairdryer	1.5 kW	Electric fire	2.0 kW
Radio	4 W	Lawn mower	1.3 kW

a What is meant by the 'power rating of the electric kettle is 2.4 kW'?

_____ [2 marks]

b Calculate the total energy used in when the hairdryer is switched on for 15 minutes.

_____ kWh [3 marks]

D–C

4 a The reading on an electricity meter is 32 456 in December. The previous reading in September was 31 667. How much electricity was used in those three months?
A 789
B 64 123
C 31 667
D 32 456 [1 mark]

b Electricity costs 10p per kWh. The cost of electricity when 347 kWh are used is
A 347p
B 34.7p
C £3470
D £34.70 [1 mark]

c The power of a DVD player is 600 W. It is switched on for 60 seconds. The energy used in Joules is
A 10
B 36
C 36 000
D 600 [1 mark]

d Digital TV set-up boxes use less energy on stand by than when they are in use. This means that when the box is on stand by
A no energy is being wasted.
B the amount of wasted energy is reduced.
C the wasted energy does not change.
D the box cannot overheat. [1 mark]

D–C

B–A*

The National Grid

D–C

1 Match words, **A**, **B**, **C** and **D**, with the statements **1 – 4** in the table.

A step-up transformer   **B** National Grid   **C** power station   **D** substation

1	a network of power stations and cables carrying electricity across the country
2	place where electricity is generated
3	part of the National Grid that reduces the voltage of electricity
4	device that increases the voltage

1	2	3	4

[4 marks]

D–C

2 Match numbers, **A**, **B**, **C** and **D**, with the spaces **1 – 4** in the table.

A 6   **B** 3   **C** 2   **D** 4

1	2	3	4

Item	Power (watts)	Current (amps)	Voltage (volts)
Electric blanket	920	**1**	230
Remote controlled car	12	2	**2**
Television	460	**3**	230
Torch	**4**	0.5	6

[4 marks]

B–A*

3 a What type of current is supplied from a battery?

_____ [1 mark]

b Explain how this current is different from the current supplied by power stations.

_____ [2 marks]

D–C

c Explain why energy losses are reduced if electricity is transported at a very high voltage.

_____ [2 marks]

Generating electricity

D–C

4 a Anna's bicycle has a **dynamo** attached to its lights. A dynamo is used to change kinetic energy into electrical energy.

   i Why do the lights shine when the wheels are turning?

_____ [1 mark]

   ii Write down the energy change that takes place in the dynamo.

_____ energy → _____ energy   [1 mark]

b The diagram shows a coil of wire attached to a sensitive ammeter. When a current flows, the needle moves.

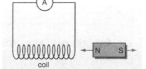

   i Why does the needle flick if the magnet moves into the coil?

_____ [1 mark]

   ii Explain why a larger current is registered when the magnet moves faster.

_____ [1 mark]

Power stations

1 Match words, **A**, **B**, **C** and **D**, with the statements **1 – 4** in the table.

A biomass   **B** coal   **C** hydroelectricity   **D** uranium

1	a non-renewable fuel
2	a nuclear fuel
3	a renewable energy source
4	a renewable fuel

1	2	3	4

D–C

[4 marks]

2 The diagram shows how electricity is generated in a power station.

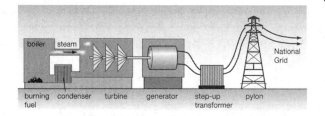

a Write down the energy change that takes place
  i in the boiler.

_____   [2 marks]

  ii in the generator.

_____   [1 mark]

b Explain **one** reason why combined cycle gas power stations are more efficient than coal burning power stations.

_____
_____   [2 marks]

c How do **combined heat and power** stations use the waste energy to increase efficiency?

_____
_____   [1 mark]

d Describe **one** way that domestic waste can be used to generate electricity.

_____
_____   [2 marks]

D–C
B–A*

Renewable energy

3 France has a large tidal power station.
  a Explain how the tidal power station generates electricity.

_____
_____
_____   [3 marks]

  b Write down **one disadvantage** of using tidal power stations.

_____   [1 mark]

  c Explain **one** way that the Sun's heat can be used to generate electricity.

_____
_____
_____   [3 marks]

D–C
B–A*

Electricity and the environment

D–C

1 a Write down **two** harmful effects of burning fossil fuels.

_____ [2 marks]

b Explain why wind turbines are useful in remote areas.

_____

_____ [2 marks]

Making comparisons

D–C

2 a Sienna is comparing the effects on the environment of coal-fired power stations and nuclear power stations.

 i Which of these power stations release greenhouse gases?

_____ [1 mark]

 ii Which of the fuels used in these power stations, will run out one day?

_____ [2 marks]

b Power stations need to be located on suitable sites. Write down **three factors** that a company may consider before choosing a site for a coal-fired power station.

_____

_____ [3 marks]

B–A*

c Sometimes there are unwanted effects when siting hydroelectric power stations. Explain why rotting vegetation caused when a site repeatedly floods and then experiences drought may contribute to greenhouse gases.

_____

_____ [3 marks]

D–C

3 Match words, **A**, **B**, **C** and **D**, with the numbers **1 – 4** in the sentences.

A cheap   **B** efficient   **C** flexible   **D** reliable

Fossil fuel power stations are designed to waste less energy, so they are more ____ **1** ____.

At the moment, fossil fuels are ____ **2** ____ but their price will rise when supplies get low.

Solar cells cannot generate electricity when it is dark or cloudy because they are not ____ **3** ____.

In some places hydroelectric stations can provide electricity in seconds, making it very ____ **4** ____.

1	2	3	4

[4 marks]

D–C

4 a What **two** things affect the total cost of electricity produced?

_____ [2 marks]

b Explain why a new gas power station may cost more to build in future, but have lower running costs than existing power stations.

_____

_____ [3 marks]

B–A*

c Describe **one** other method of generating electricity direct from organic matter.

_____

_____ [3 marks]

P1a revision checklist

I know:

how heat (thermal energy) is transferred and what factors affect the rate at which heat is transferred

☐ heat energy can be transferred by conduction, convection and thermal radiation

☐ thermal conductors (e.g. metals) transfer heat energy easily; thermal insulators (e.g. plastic, glass) do not

☐ dark, dull surfaces emit and absorb thermal radiation better than shiny, light surfaces

☐ the bigger the temperature difference between an object and its surroundings, the faster the rate at which heat is transferred

what is meant by the efficient use of energy

☐ energy is never created nor destroyed; some energy is usually wasted as heat

☐ the greater the percentage of the energy that is usefully transformed in a device, the more efficient the device is

☐ how to calculate the efficiency of a device:

$$\text{efficiency} = \frac{\textbf{useful energy output}}{\textbf{total energy input}}$$

why electrical devices are so useful

☐ they transform electrical energy to whatever form of energy we need at the flick of a switch

☐ the National Grid transmits energy around the country at high voltages and low current to keep energy losses low

☐ dynamos produce electricity when coils of wire rotate inside a magnetic field

☐ how to work out the power rating of an appliance (the rate at which it transforms electrical energy)

☐ how to calculate the amount of energy transferred from the mains:

energy transferred = power × time

☐ how to calculate the cost of energy transferred from the mains:

total cost = number of kilowatt-hours × cost per kilowatt-hour

how we should generate the electricity we need

☐ we need to use more renewable energy sources, including wind, hydroelectric, tidal, wave and geothermal power

☐ most types of electricity generation have some harmful effects on people or the environment; there are also limitations on where they can be used

Uses of electromagnetic radiation

1 a Write down **three properties** that all electromagnetic waves share.

_____

_____ [3 marks]

b The diagram shows the members of the electromagnetic spectrum. Fill in the names missing on the diagram.

Radio waves	**1**	Infrared	**2**	Ultraviolet	**3**	Gamma rays

Increasing frequency

⟶

Increasing energy

⟶

1 _____   2 _____   3 _____ [3 marks]

c Match words, **A**, **B**, **C** and **D**, with the numbers **1 – 4** in the sentences.

A infrared   **B** ultraviolet   **C** visible light   **D** X-rays

____ **1** ____ are used to check baggage at airports for dangerous and illegal items. Forged bank notes show up under ____ **2** ____ light. Trespassers can be detected if they walk through ____ **3** ____ beams in buildings. Security cameras use ____ **4** ____ to take pictures in high security areas.

1	2	3	4

[4 marks]

2 Match words, **A**, **B**, **C** and **D**, with the numbers **1 – 4** in the sentences.

A gamma rays   **B** infrared   **C** radio waves   **D** ultra violet

____ **1** ____ are used for broadcasts. ____ **2** ____ are used to detect parts of the body that are warmer due to inflammation. Our skin develops a suntan when exposed to ____ **3** ____. ____ **4** ____ can be used to kill cells, and sterilise surgical instruments.

1	2	3	4

[4 marks]

Electromagnetic spectrum 1

3 a Add a label to the diagram to show one wavelength. [1 mark]

b Under the wave, add a diagram of another wave which carries more energy. [2 marks]

c Write down the relationship between frequency and energy.

_____ [1 mark]

d An electromagnetic wave is absorbed by a radio antenna, creating an alternating current. How are the frequency of the radiation and the alternating current connected?

_____ [1 mark]

Electromagnetic spectrum 2

1 Match words, **A**, **B**, **C** and **D**, with the numbers **1 – 4** in the sentences.

| **A** absorb | **B** carry | **C** reflects | **D** transmits |

All electromagnetic waves ____ **1** ____ energy. A mirror ____ **2** ____ light
so we can see an image. A window ____ **3** ____ light helping us see
during the day. Black material ____ **4** ____ light so it looks dark.

1	2	3	4

[4 marks]

2

Wave type	Wavelength	Sources	Detectors
Gamma rays	10^{-12} m	Radioactive nuclei	Geiger-Müller tube
X-rays	10^{-10} m	X-ray tubes	Geiger-Müller tube
Ultraviolet	10^{-7} m	Sun, very hot objects	Skin, photographic film, fluorescent material
Visible light	0.0005 mm	Hot objects, Sun, lasers, LEDs	Eyes, photographic film
Infrared	0.1 mm	Warm or hot objects	Skin, thermometer
Microwaves	1–10 cm	Radar, microwave ovens	Aerial, mobile phone
Radio waves	10– 1000+ m	Radio transmitters	Aerial, TV, radio

Complete these sentences using the words **absorbed**, **transmitted** or **reflected**.

a Satellites use microwaves communications because these waves are _____ by the atmosphere.

b Ultraviolet waves are _____ by our skin, causing suntan.

c White cars stay cool in the sun because infrared is _____ by the light colour.

Waves and matter

3 a What type of electromagnetic radiation is used to take shadow pictures of bones?

_____ [1 mark]

b Explain how a picture of a person's bones can be taken using electromagnetic radiation.

_____

_____

_____ [3 marks]

c Suggest **one** reason why these pictures are taken only when necessary.

_____ [1 mark]

4 a How fast does light travel? _____ [1 mark]

b What is the equation that links speed, frequency and wavelength?

_____ [1 mark]

c Calculate
i the wavelength of radio waves if their frequency is 300 000 Hz.

_____

_____ [2 marks]

ii the frequency of microwaves if their wavelength is 0.03 m. Include the units.

_____

_____ [3 marks]

Dangers of radiation

1 Match words, **A**, **B**, **C** and **D**, with the numbers **1 – 4** in the sentences.

   A absorb   **B** burn   **C** ionise   **D** kill

Cells ____ **1** ____ many types of radiation which can damage them.

High doses of gamma rays ____ **2** ____ cancer cells.

Low doses of X-rays and gamma rays ____ **3** ____ cells, damaging them.

Infrared radiation and microwaves ____ **4** ____ cells.

1	2	3	4

[4 marks]

2 Rachel has put sun-block on to protect her skin before she goes out in the Sun.

  a What type of electromagnetic radiation does sun-block protect her from?

[1 mark]

  b Write down **three** risks from too much exposure to this type of radiation.

[3 marks]

  c Explain why darker skins are less likely to be damaged by the Sun's radiation.

[3 marks]

  d Explain what effect the shorter wavelength electromagnetic waves have on the molecules in cells and why this may cause cancer.

[1 mark]

Telecommunications

3 a What is the name given the type of signal shown in figure A?

[1 mark]

  b Explain how digital signals carrying a cable TV programme are sent.

A

B

[2 marks]

  c Suggest **one** reason why underground telephone cables are no longer being laid.

[1 mark]

  d Many communication links are now made using satellite links.
Write down **two advantages** of using satellite communications.

[2 marks]

Fibre optics: digital signals

1 a Explain how an **optical fibre** is used to send digital signals.

_____

_____ [2 marks]

b The diagram shows light travelling down an optical fibre.

    i Continue the path of the light ray until it emerges from the optical fibre. [3 marks]

    ii What is the **name** given to the process that occurs inside the optical fibre?

_____ [1 mark]

c State **two advantages** of using digital technology to store information on car driving licences.

_____

_____ [2 marks]

D–C

B–A*

Radioactivity

2 Match words, **A**, **B**, **C** and **D**, with the arrows **1 – 4** in the diagram.

A electron

B neutron

C nucleus

D proton

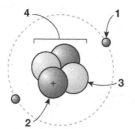

1	2	3	4

[4 marks]

D–C

3 The table gives some information about different atoms.

Element	Number of protons	Number of neutrons
A	6	6
B	6	7
C	7	7
D	8	8

a Which elements are isotopes of each other?

_____ [1 mark]

b How many electrons are orbiting the nucleus of element A? _____ [1 mark]

c What is the mass number of element C? _____ [1 mark]

d Explain what is meant by **radioactive decay**.

_____

_____ [2 marks]

D–C

Alpha, beta and gamma rays 1

D–C

1 a Explain what is meant by an **alpha particle**.

_____ [2 marks]

b Alpha particles are very ionising. Inside the body, they damage cells. Explain why alpha particles are unlikely to cause damage to people in most cases.

_____ [1 mark]

c Write down **two** uses for alpha radiation.

_____ [2 marks]

d Why are gamma rays **less ionising** than alpha particles?

_____ [2 marks]

B–A*

2 a Which **two** types of radiation are deflected by electric fields?

_____ [2 marks]

b Give **one** reason why these types of radiation are deflected in different directions.

_____ [1 mark]

Background radiation 1

D–C

3 a Background radiation is
A very rare.
B found only in a few places.
C found all around us.
D only caused by natural sources. [1 mark]

b Radon gas is found in some areas of the United Kingdom. It is
A not a health risk.
B a health risk causing raised levels of lung cancer in these regions.
C caused by man-made sources only.
D not possible to change your exposure to radon gas. [1 mark]

c Cosmic radiation is caused by the Sun. It is
A mainly absorbed by the atmosphere.
B a significant health risk on all flights.
C not a health risk.
D the same intensity at sea level and on high altitude flights. [1 mark]

d Radiation badges are worn
A to protect people from exposure to radioactivity.
B as a source of radioactivity.
C to give an instant read-out of exposure to radioactivity.
D to monitor exposure to radioactivity over a period of time. [1 mark]

B–A*

4 Lindi is using a Geiger counter to monitor a radioactive source. Explain why

a there is a reading even when the source is stored in a lead lined container.

_____ [1 mark]

b the readings from the source fluctuate.

_____ [1 mark]

Half-life

1 a After two half-lives, in a radioactive sample
    A all of the atoms will decay.
    B none of the atoms will decay.
    C exactly half of the atoms will decay.
    D about half of the atoms will decay.
    [1 mark]

b The length of a sample's half-life depends on
    A the type of material that is decaying.
    B the temperature the sample is kept in.
    C the pressure the sample feels.
    D the country the sample was found in.
    [1 mark]

c The half-life of a sample is the time taken for
    A half of its mass to disappear.
    B its original activity to fall to half.
    C half of the samples measured to decay completely.
    D its count rate to change.
    [1 mark]

d A sample of cobalt has a half-life of 5 years, and its count rate is 1200 counts per second. After 15 years, the count rate is
    A 600   **B** 300   **C** 150   **D** 0
    [1 mark]

D–C

2 a Explain what is meant by **half-life**.

_____

_____ [3 marks]

b What types of materials can be dated using **radiocarbon dating**?

_____ [1 mark]

c The proportion of radioactive carbon in a wooden arrow has been measured. Explain whether the proportion of radioactive carbon in an arrow 10 000 years old will be more or less than that found in an arrow made from modern wood.

_____

_____ [2 marks]

d The proportion of radioactive carbon in a wooden arrow has been measured. Explain whether the proportion of radioactive carbon in an arrow 10 000 years old will be more or less than that found in an arrow made from modern wood.

_____

_____ [3 marks]

D–C

B–A*

Uses of nuclear radiation

3 The diagram shows one method of controlling the thickness of paper in a factory.

a Write down **one** reason why is it important to monitor the thickness.

_____

_____ [1 mark]

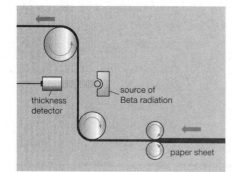

thickness
detector

source of
Beta radiation

paper sheet

b Why is alpha radiation not used to detect the thickness of the paper?

_____ [1 mark]

c Explain how the machine should adjust the rollers if the amount of radiation reaching the detector gets smaller.

_____

_____ [2 marks]

D–C

Safety first

1 a A person is working with a radioactive sample. Which precaution will make no difference to her exposure?

A using tongs

B putting the sample back in its case after use

C wearing a lead apron

D reducing the temperature of the room [1 mark]

b Special badges are worn by people who work with radioactivity so that

A the radioactivity is neutralised.

B the amount of radioactivity received can be measured.

C their colleagues know that they are authorised.

D they do not develop cancer. [1 mark]

c When radioactivity is absorbed, which of these effects never occurs?

A infection

B cell mutation

C absorption of energy

D ionisation [1 mark]

d One effect of exposure to radiation is to

A selectively repair previous cell damage.

B ionise cells.

C ionise DNA molecules in cells.

D make cells radioactive. [1 mark]

Searching space

2 Telescopes are used to examine the night sky.

a Explain why a reflecting telescope produces better images than a simple optical telescope.

_____

_____ [2 marks]

b The Hubble telescope is a space telescope. Explain what is meant by a **space telescope**.

_____

_____ [2 marks]

c Describe **two advantages** of having a telescope in orbit.

_____

_____ [2 marks]

3 Match words, **A**, **B**, **C** and **D**, with the numbers **1 – 4** in the sentences.

A gamma   **B** infrared   **C** ultraviolet   **D** visible

We can see ____ **1** ____ light from stars using binoculars. ____ **2** ____ rays

emitted by neutron stars can be detected using space-based telescopes.

These are also used to detect ____ **3** ____ radiation from

red giants and ____ **4** ____ radiation from quasars.

1	2	3	4

[4 marks]

Gravity

1 Match words, **A**, **B**, **C** and **D**, with the numbers **1 – 4** in the sentences.

A force   **B** gravity   **C** mass   **D** separation

All objects are attracted to each other because of ____ **1** ____.

The attractive ____ **2** ____ is greater if the ____ **3** ____ of the

objects is small or if the ____ **4** ____ of the objects is big.

1	2	3	4

[4 marks]

2 The diagram shows how one spacecraft used gravity to travel across the Solar System.

  a Explain what caused the spacecraft to change direction as it passed the different planets.

    _____

    _____

    [1 mark]

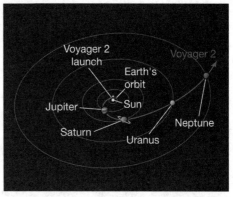

  b Explain why astronauts in an orbiting spacecraft feel weightless.

    _____

    [1 mark]

Birth of a star

3 The statements, **A**, **B**, **C** and **D**, describe the stages in the formation of a star. Put them in the correct order, matching the statements with the correct places **1 – 4** in the boxes.

A gas molecules are pulled together by gravity to form a cloud
B nuclear fusion starts
C the cloud attracts more particles and gets larger
D the core of the nebula heats up dramatically

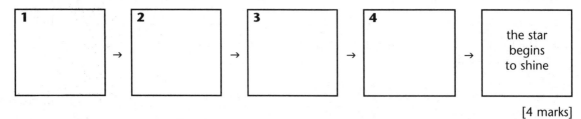

[4 marks]

4 a Explain why nuclear fusion results in heavier elements forming.

    _____

    _____

    [2 marks]

  b Explain how we know that the Solar System must have contained pieces of a bigger star than our Sun.

    _____

    _____

    [2 marks]

Formation of the Solar System

D–C

1 The diagram shows one idea of how
the Solar System was formed.

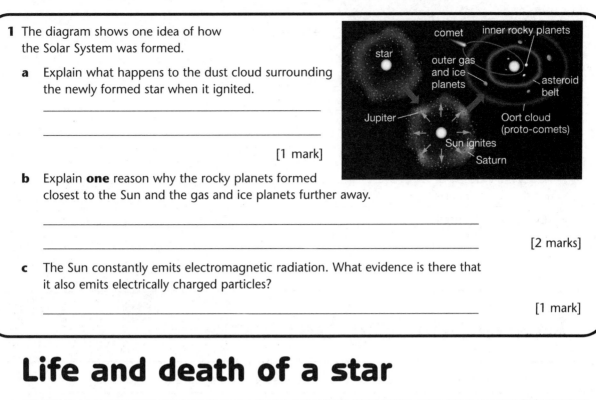

a Explain what happens to the dust cloud surrounding
the newly formed star when it ignited.

_____

_____

[1 mark]

b Explain **one** reason why the rocky planets formed
closest to the Sun and the gas and ice planets further away.

_____

_____

[2 marks]

B–A*

c The Sun constantly emits electromagnetic radiation. What evidence is there that
it also emits electrically charged particles?

_____

[1 mark]

Life and death of a star

D–C

2 Match words, **A**, **B**, **C** and **D**, with the numbers **1 – 4** in the sentences.

A black hole   **B** neutron star   **C** red giant   **D** supernova

A star the size of our Sun will eventually expand to form a ____ **1** ____.

Stars larger than our Sun become red supergiants, which collapse and

explode as a spectacular ____ **2** ____. The core remains an incredibly

dense ____ **3** ____. If the star was very massive, a ____ **4** ____ remains instead.

1	2	3	4

[4 marks]

D–C

3 Stars begin as a cloud of dust and gas which are crushed by gravity until nuclear
fusion reactions begin.

a Explain why the Sun is constantly losing mass.

_____ [1 mark]

b Write down the three stages that a star, like our Sun, will go through before it
eventually dies.

_____ → _____ → _____ [3 marks]

B–A*

c What **two** factors are balanced when a star is in the stable phase?

_____

_____

[2 marks]

d How do these two forces control the life cycle of the star?

_____

_____

_____

[3 marks]

In the beginning

1 a When is the Big Bang thought to have taken place?

_____

[1 mark]

b Explain what is meant by the **Big Bang theory**.

_____

_____

[2 marks]

c Explain how heavier elements were created from **quarks**.

_____

_____

[3 marks]

d Why is the presence of background microwave radiation additional evidence for the Big Bang?

_____

[2 marks]

D–C

B–A*

The expanding Universe

2 Astronomers looking at distant galaxies have noticed an effect they called the red shift.

a Explain what is meant by the **red shift**.

_____

_____

[2 marks]

b What does the red shift tell astronomers about the **motion** of galaxies?

_____

[1 mark]

D–C

3 a Galaxies close to us have a smaller red shift than galaxies further away. This tells us that galaxies are moving

A at the same speed.

B away from us at different speeds.

C towards us at different speeds.

D slowly. [1 mark]

b A spectroscope is used to

A measure your heart.

B display the electromagnetic spectrum.

C split light into different colours.

D rejoin light that has been split up.

[1 mark]

c An element emits a unique pattern of light when it is

A heated.

B looked at under high pressure.

C reacting with other elements.

D cooled. [1 mark]

d The change in the colour of light from galaxies occurs because of

A the great distance the light travels.

B the different temperatures of the stars.

C interference from our atmosphere.

D the change in wavelength of the light.

[1 mark]

D–C

4 a It is thought that the Universe is still expanding as a result of the Big Bang. Explain what is meant by the **Big Crunch** and what it depends on.

_____

_____

[3 marks]

b State **two** other possible futures for the Universe.

_____

_____

[2 marks]

B–A*

P1b revision checklist

I know:

what the uses and hazards of the waves that form the electromagnetic spectrum are

☐ from longest to shortest wavelength: radio waves, microwaves, infrared, visible light, ultraviolet, X-rays, gamma rays

☐ electromagnetic radiation has many uses in communication, e.g. radio, TV, satellites, cable and mobile phone networks

☐ communication signals can be digital or analogue

☐ some forms of electromagnetic radiation can damage living cells: ionising radiation (ultraviolet, X-rays and gamma rays) can cause cancer

☐ electromagnetic waves obey the wave formula:

wave speed = **frequency** × **wavelength**

what the uses and dangers of emissions from radioactive substances are

☐ the uses and hazards of radioactive substances (which emit alpha particles, beta particles and gamma rays) depend on the wavelength and frequency of the radiation they emit

☐ background radiation is all around us, e.g. granite rocks can emit gamma rays and form radioactive radon gas

☐ the relative ionising power, penetration through materials and range in air of alpha, beta and gamma radiations

☐ the activity (count) rate of a radioisotope is measured as its half-life

about the origins of the Universe and how it continues to change

☐ the Universe is still expanding; in the beginning, matter and space expanded violently and rapidly from a very small initial point, i.e. the Big Bang

☐ red shift indicates that galaxies are moving apart; the further away a galaxy, the faster it is moving away from us

☐ telescopes on Earth and in space give us information about the Solar System and the galaxies in the Universe

Cells

1 The diagram shows a plant cell.

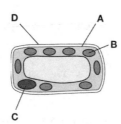

D–C

a Name parts B and C.

B _____ C _____ [2 marks]

b Describe the functions of parts A and D.

A _____

D_____ [2 marks]

c Describe the functions of each of these organelles.

Ribosomes _____

Mitochondria _____ [2 marks]

Specialised cells

2 The diagram shows a ciliated cell.
Cells like this are found in
the lining of the trachea and
bronchi leading down to the lungs.

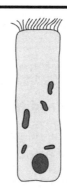

D–C

a Describe the function of ciliated cells.

_____ [1 mark]

b State **two** ways in which ciliated cells are adapted for their function.

1_____

2_____ [2 marks]

3 The diagram shows the tip of a plant root, magnified.

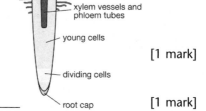

B–A*

a What is the function of root hair cells?

_____

_____ [1 mark]

b Suggest how their shape adapts them for their function.

_____ [1 mark]

c Suggest **two** ways in which the young cells in the plant root would differ from
the cell shown in Question **1**.

1_____

2_____ [2 marks]

Diffusion 1

1 a Complete the definition of diffusion.

Diffusion is the spreading of the _____ of a _____ , or of any

substance in solution. This results in a _____ movement from a region

where they are in a _____ concentration. [4 marks]

b Explain why diffusion happens faster when the temperature is higher.

_____

_____ [2 marks]

2 The diagram shows a cell.

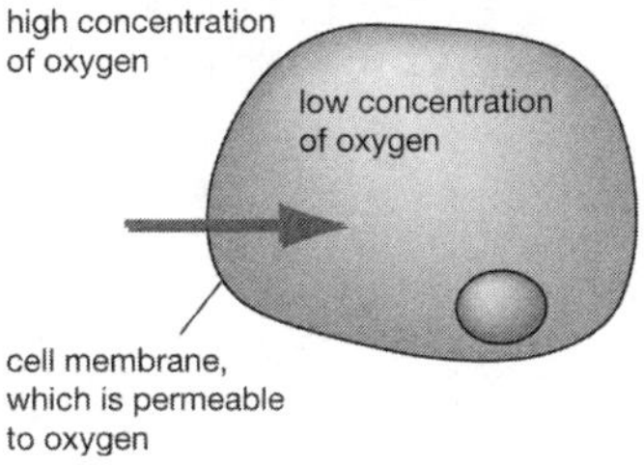

high concentration of oxygen

low concentration of oxygen

cell membrane, which is permeable to oxygen

a Name the part of the cell that uses oxygen. (These parts are not shown on

the diagram.) _____ [1 mark]

b Explain why oxygen diffuses into the cell more rapidly, when these parts are working faster.

_____

_____ [2 marks]

c The lungs are full of tiny spaces called alveoli, which contain air that has been breathed in. Blood that has travelled around the body is pumped from the heart to the lungs. It flows through capillaries that are wrapped closely around the alveoli. Explain why oxygen diffuses into the blood, and carbon dioxide diffuses out of the blood, in the lungs.

_____

_____ [2 marks]

Diffusion 2

3 The cells inside a plant leaf photosynthesise during the daytime. There are tiny holes in the underside of the leaf called stomata. Gases are able to diffuse in and out of the leaf through the stomata.

a Which gas will diffuse **into** the leaf during the daytime?

_____ [1 mark]

b Explain why this gas diffuses into the leaf.

_____

_____ [2 marks]

c Suggest how the rate of diffusion of this gas might differ on a bright, sunny day compared with a dull day. Explain your answer.

_____

_____ [2 marks]

Osmosis 1

1 Complete the definition of osmosis.

Osmosis is the _____ of _____

from a _____ to a more concentrated solution through a

_____ permeable membrane. **[4 marks]**

D–C

2 The diagram shows a piece of Visking tubing containing sugar solution. The tubing is in a beaker of water.

- glass tubing
- dilute sugar solution
- Visking tubing – a partially permeable membrane
- concentrated sugar solution

a Explain why the level of liquid in the tubing rises. Your answer should refer to water molecules, sugar molecules, and the Visking tubing membrane.

_____

_____

_____ **[3 marks]**

b Suggest **two** ways in which you could speed up the rate at which the level of the liquid rises in the tube.

1_____

2_____ **[2 marks]**

D–C

B–A*

Osmosis 2

3 The diagram shows an animal cell that has been placed in water.

- distilled water
- cytoplasm – a fairly concentrated solution
- cell membrane – a partially permeable membrane

a What will eventually happen to the cell? Explain your answer.

_____

_____ **[2 marks]**

b Explain why this does **not** happen to a plant cell in pure water even though water enters the cell by osmosis.

_____

_____ **[2 marks]**

c Look carefully at this plant cell.
What has made the cell look like this? Explain your answer.

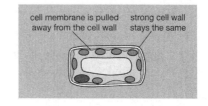

cell membrane is pulled away from the cell wall   strong cell wall stays the same

_____

_____

_____

[3 marks]

D–C

B–A*

Photosynthesis

1 a Write the word equation for photosynthesis.

_____

[2 marks]

b Describe the role of chlorophyll in photosynthesis.

_____

_____

[2 marks]

c The first substance that plants make in photosynthesis is glucose. Name **two** substances that the plant can make from the glucose, and state the function of each.

1st Substance _____

Function _____

2nd Substance _____

Function _____

[4 marks]

Leaves

2 a This diagram shows the internal structure of a leaf as it would look under a microscope.

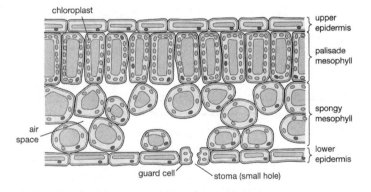

i Explain how the **position** of the palisade mesophyll cells helps them to carry out their function.

_____

_____

[2 marks]

ii Name **one** type of cell, labelled in the diagram, that cannot photosynthesise.

_____

[1 mark]

b Many of the cells in the leaf contain stores of starch. Explain why starch is better than glucose for storage purposes.

_____

_____

[2 marks]

Limiting factors

1 Grace wants to find out if a water plant makes oxygen more rapidly when it has more light.

She put a piece of pond weed into a test tube of water. She took it into a room where the light was dim. She counted the number of bubbles that the pond weed gave off in one minute. She did this twice more at the same light intensity. She then repeated this at three other light intensities.

The table shows her results. The higher the number for light intensity, the brighter the light.

Light intensity	Number of bubbles given off in one minute			
	1st try	**2nd try**	**3rd try**	**Average**
1	6	9	10	8.3
2	16	18	20	18.0
3	28	27	29	28.0
4	30	32	34	

a Fill in the empty box in the table. [1 mark]

b What was the dependent variable in Grace's experiment? _____ [1 mark]

c Grace's teacher says that Grace's results suggest she should let the plant settle down at each new light intensity before beginning to count the bubbles. Explain how Grace's results support this suggestion.

_____ [2 marks]

d Grace thinks that her results show that light can be a limiting factor for photosynthesis. Do you agree? Explain your answer.

_____ [2 marks]

e Predict what Grace's results would be if she increased the light intensity to 8 units. Explain your answer.

_____ [2 marks]

B–A*

B–A*

2 Gardeners often burn paraffin in heaters in a glasshouse where tomatoes are being grown. How might this help the tomatoes to grow faster and produce a better crop?

_____ [2 marks]

Healthy plants

D–C

3 a Complete the sentences.

Plants obtain mineral ions from the _____. They need nitrate ions for

producing _____ acids, which are then used to form _____.

They need _____ ions for making chlorophyll. [4 marks]

B–A*

b This graph shows how adding fertiliser containing nitrate to the soil affected the growth of wheat in a field.

i Explain why adding nitrate-containing fertiliser up to 150 kg per hectare increased the yield of grain.

_____

[2 marks]

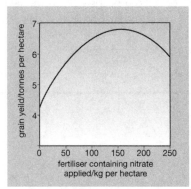

ii Suggest why adding more than 150 kg per hectare decreased the yield of grain.

_____

[2 marks]

Food chains

D–C

1 a Energy enters a food chain as solar energy, in light. In what form is the energy passed along the food chain?

_____

[1 mark]

b Explain why green plants only capture a small part of the solar energy that reaches them.

_____

_____

[2 marks]

B–A*

c The efficiency of energy transfer from light energy to chemical energy in a plant is about 20%.

i Name the part of a cell where this energy transfer takes place.

_____

[1 mark]

ii Sunlight containing 1000 units of light energy falls onto a leaf. Calculate the quantity of energy that will be transformed to chemical energy in the leaf.

_____

[1 mark]

D–C

2 Mammals and birds keep their body temperature constant even when the temperature around them is low.

Explain why this means that energy transfer from mammals or birds to the next organism in a food chain is not very efficient.

_____

_____

[2 marks]

Biomass

B–A*

3 The diagram shows a pyramid of biomass.

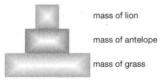

mass of lion

mass of antelope

mass of grass

a Write the name of the trophic level next to each step in the pyramid.

_____

[1 mark]

b Several hundred caterpillars live on a cabbage plant. They are eaten by small birds, which in turn are eaten by sparrowhawks.

i Sketch a pyramid of biomass for this food chain.

[1 mark]

ii Explain why the pyramid is the shape that you have drawn it.

_____

_____

[2 marks]

Food production

1 Some farmers rear chickens indoors, in heated sheds. Explain how this can help to reduce energy losses and improve the efficiency of the production of chickens.

_____

_____

[2 marks]

2 It has been suggested that, if we all became vegetarians, we could produce more food on each hectare of land. Discuss this suggestion.

_____

_____

_____

_____

[4 marks]

The cost of good food

3 Hens that are kept to produce eggs may be kept in three different ways:

Ways of keeping hens	Freedom of hens	Cost of a box of 6 eggs
Free range	Can roam outside	99p
In barns	Can move around freely	73p
In battery cages	Cannot move freely	54p

a Explain why free range eggs are more expensive than barn eggs and battery eggs.

_____

_____

[2 marks]

b Suggest why many people buy free range eggs even though they are more expensive than battery eggs.

_____

_____

[2 marks]

4 It has been calculated that growing tomatoes in Britain in winter is more expensive and does more damage to the environment than importing tomatoes from Spain.

a Explain how transporting tomatoes from Spain could harm the environment.

_____

_____

[2 marks]

b Suggest why growing tomatoes in Britain in the winter might damage the environment even more than this.

_____

_____

[2 marks]

Death and decay

1 Karen and Joanna did an investigation to compare the rate of decay in two different areas of soil. Area A was inside a wood. Area B was on a flower bed.

They cut some graph paper into two 10 cm x 10 cm squares. They place one piece of paper on the soil in area A, and the other in area B. They weighed the paper down with pebbles. They looked at the paper after six weeks, and counted how many of of the 1 cm x 1 cm squares on the paper had decayed.

They found that 45 of the 1 cm x 1 cm squares had disappeared from the paper in area A, and 34 of the squares had disappeared in area B.

a How many small 1 cm x 1 cm squares were there on each piece of graph paper at the start of the experiment? _____ [1 mark]

b State the percentage of paper that had decayed in each area after six weeks.

Area A _____ Area B _____ [1 mark]

c What caused the paper to decay?

_____ [1 mark]

d Suggest reasons for the results that the students obtained.

_____

_____ [2 marks]

e **i** What was the independent variable in this experiment?

_____ [1 mark]

ii What was the dependent variable?

_____ [1 mark]

f How could the students have made their results more reliable?

_____ [1 mark]

Cycles

2 a Complete the sentences.

Organisms such as earthworms, which eat dead leaves and other plant remains, are called

_____ feeders. They help to recycle the materials in the plant remains,

so that they become available to other members of the _____ of organisms

in the ecosystem. For example, they release some of the carbon in the leaves back into the air,

in the form of carbon dioxide, by the process of _____. [3 marks]

b Which of the organisms in a food web may be eaten by detritus feeders?

_____ [1 mark]

c Explain why detritus feeders are said to be **consumers** in a food chain.

_____

_____ [2 marks]

The carbon cycle 1

1 a The Martian atmosphere is mostly carbon dioxide. If pressurised, it would become suitable for plant life. Suggest what is most likely to be the limiting factor for photosynthesis on Mars if plants were growing in a pressurised atmosphere.

_____ [1 mark]

b Explain why humans living on Mars would need to grow plants inside the enclosed environments where they would live.

_____

_____ [2 marks]

The carbon cycle 2

2 The diagram shows parts of the carbon cycle. The numbers indicate how many billions of tonnes of carbon pass along each pathway in one year.

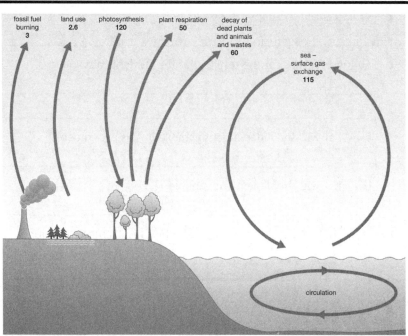

fossil fuel burning **3**   land use **2.6**   photosynthesis **120**   plant respiration **50**   decay of dead plants and animals and wastes **60**   sea – surface gas exchange **115**   circulation

a Explain how decay of dead plants and animals releases carbon dioxide into the air.

_____

_____ [2 marks]

b Calculate the difference between the quantity of carbon removed from the air by photosynthesis by land plants and the quantity returned to the air by plant respiration.

_____ [1 mark]

c Explain how this supports the idea that deforestation could contribute to global warming.

_____

_____ [3 marks]

d 'Land use' refers to the disturbance of soil, which contains a lot of carbon locked up in the form of carbon compounds. Using what you know about decomposers, suggest how this carbon got into the soil.

_____

_____ [2 marks]

e Suggest what is meant by **sea surface gas exchange**.

_____

_____ [2 marks]

B2a revision checklist

I know:

what animals and plants are built from

☐ animal cells and plant cells have a membrane, cytoplasm and a nucleus; plant cells also have a cell wall and may have a vacuole and chloroplasts

☐ in multicellular organisms, different cells are specialised for different functions

☐ the chemical reactions inside cells are controlled by enzymes

how dissolved substances get into and out of cells

☐ diffusion is the net movement of particles of gas, or substances dissolved in a solution, from a region of high concentration to a region of lower concentration

☐ oxygen required for respiration passes through cell membranes by diffusion

☐ osmosis is the diffusion of water molecules through a partially permeable membrane

how plants obtain the food they need to live and grow

☐ green plants use chlorophyll to trap light energy from the Sun to photosynthesise

☐ leaves are specially adapted for photosynthesis – they can be broad, flat, thin and have lots of stomata

☐ the rate of photosynthesis is affected by light intensity, carbon dioxide concentration and temperature

☐ mineral salts in the soil are used to make proteins or chlorophyll; lack of a mineral ion results in a deficiency symptom in a plant

what happens to energy and biomass at each stage in a food chain

☐ energy passes along food chains but some energy is lost at every stage

☐ the shorter the food chain, the less energy is lost

☐ the mass of biomass at each stage in a food chain is less than it was at the previous stage; this can be shown in a pyramid of biomass

☐ reducing energy loss increases the efficiency of food production

☐ decomposers and detritus feeders feed on dead organisms and their waste

Enzymes – biological catalysts

1 Complete these sentences.

Enzymes are biological _____. They are _____ molecules.

Each kind of enzyme only works on a particular kind of _____ , which fits

perfectly into a fold in the enzyme called the _____ site. **[4 marks]**

D–C

2 This graph shows how temperature affects the activity of an enzyme.

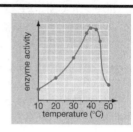

a Using what you know about rates of reaction, explain why the activity of the enzyme increases as the temperature is increased from 10 °C to 20 °C.

_____

_____ **[3 marks]**

b Lucy says that the enzyme stops working at high temperatures because it has been killed. Explain why Lucy is wrong, and give the correct explanation for the shape of the graph at temperatures above 40 °C.

_____

_____ **[3 marks]**

D–C

Enzymes and digestion

3 The diagram shows the sites of production of some of the enzymes that help with digestion.

a Name **two** organs, shown on the diagram, where amylase is produced.

1 _____   2 _____

[2 marks]

b What does amylase do?

_____

_____ **[1 mark]**

c Protease enzymes and hydrochloric acid are produced in the stomach. Sketch a graph, with pH on the *x* axis, to show how you would expect pH to affect the activity of the protease enzyme. **[3 marks]**

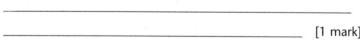

mouth
salivary glands
oesophagus
liver
stomach
gall bladder
pancreas
small intestines
large intestine
appendix
rectum
anus

D–C

B–A*

d The enzymes that are found in the small intestine require a pH that is neutral or slightly alkaline. Explain how bile helps to provide these conditions.

_____

_____ **[2 marks]**

D–C

Enzymes at home

1 a Explain how proteases in biological washing powders can help to remove blood stains from clothes.

_____

_____ [2 marks]

b Many of the enzymes that are used in biological washing powders have been obtained from bacteria that are adapted to live in hot springs, at temperatures up to 80 °C. Suggest why these enzymes are especially useful in washing powders.

_____

_____ [2 marks]

c When biological washing powders were first introduced, some people found that they harmed their hands. Now, in most biological washing powders, the enzymes are inside tiny particles surrounded by a harmless covering.

Suggest how biological washing powders could harm people's hands if the enzymes were not enclosed like this.

_____

_____ [2 marks]

Enzymes and industry

2 Read this information about a new variety of potato.

> Potatoes contain starch. A new, genetically modified, breed of potato has been produced that contains genes for making the enzymes amylase, maltase and isomerase.
>
> The enzymes begin to work when the temperature reaches about 40 °C, so the GM potatoes produce fructose when they are cooked. The cooked potatoes can be mashed and used as a source of fructose in the food industry.

a Explain what is meant by **genetically modified**.

_____

_____ [2 marks]

b Complete this flow diagram to show how fructose is produced in the GM potatoes, by writing the names of the missing enzymes.

| starch | $\longrightarrow$ | maltose | $\xrightarrow{\text{maltase}}$ | glucose | $\longrightarrow$ | fructose |

[2 marks]

c Fructose is twice as sweet as sucrose. Explain why this makes fructose useful in the food industry.

_____ [2 marks]

d Suggest why the potatoes do not make fructose until they are heated to 40 °C.

_____ [1 mark]

e Discuss why some people might not want to eat food made from fructose made by GM potatoes.

_____ [2 marks]

Respiration and energy

1 a Name the waste product of aerobic respiration.

_____ [1 mark]

b In which cells is this waste product made?

_____ [1 mark]

c Sperm cells contain a large number of mitochondria. With reference to respiration, explain why this is so.

_____

_____ [2 marks]

D–C

Removing waste: lungs

2 The table shows the approximate composition of inhaled air and exhaled air.

Name of gas	In inhaled air (approximate %)	In exhaled air (approximate %)
Carbon dioxide	0.04	4
Oxygen	21	
Nitrogen		79
Water vapour	Variable	High

a Complete the table by writing in values for the percentage of oxygen in exhaled air and the percentage of nitrogen in inhaled air. [2 marks]

b Explain why there is less oxygen in exhaled air than in inhaled air.

_____

_____ [2 marks]

c Using what you know about diffusion, explain why there is still quite a lot of oxygen in the air that we breathe out.

_____

_____

_____

_____ [4 marks]

d Predict what would happen to the concentration of carbon dioxide in exhaled air when a person is exercising vigorously. Explain your prediction.

_____

_____ [2 marks]

D–C

B–A*

Removing waste: liver and kidneys

1 The kidneys filter the blood and allow some of the substances to pass out of the body in urine. The table shows the concentrations of six substances in the blood and in urine.

Substance	Found in blood plasma (%)	Found in urine (%)
Water	92	95
Amino acids	0.05	0
Proteins	8	0
Glucose	0.1	0
Salt	0.37	0.6
Urea	0.03	2

a Explain the difference between the concentration of urea in blood plasma and in urine.

_____ [1 mark]

b Suggest why the kidneys do not allow glucose to pass out of the body in urine.

_____

_____ [2 marks]

c Salt is made up of sodium ions and chloride ions. The kidneys are able to adjust the quantity of these ions that are lost in urine. Suggest how this can help to keep the ion content of the body constant.

_____

_____ [2 marks]

Homeostasis

2 When there is too much water in the body, the kidneys excrete large amounts of dilute urine. When there is not enough, they excrete small amounts of concentrated urine.

a State **two** ways in which the body loses water, other than in urine.

1_____

2_____ [2 marks]

b Explain why a person's kidneys produce less urine on hot days than on cold days.

_____

_____ [2 marks]

c State **two** other factors, apart from water, that are kept constant inside the body.

1_____

2_____ [2 marks]

3 Animals that live in fresh water, such as fish, produce very large volumes of dilute urine. Using what you know about osmosis, suggest why this is.

_____

_____ [2 marks]

Keeping warm, staying cool

1 a Suggest why cells cannot work properly if the core body temperature gets too high.

_____ [2 marks]

b Describe how the body monitors temperature.

_____ [2 marks]

c The diagram shows the appearance of the skin when the body is too hot.

i Explain how sweating helps the body to lose heat.

_____ [2 marks]

ii What do the arterioles supplying the skin capillaries with blood do when the body is too hot?

_____ [1 mark]

iii Explain how this helps the body to lose heat.

_____ [2 marks]

D–C

B–A*

Treating diabetes

2 Andrew has diabetes. His body does not produce insulin.

a Describe what would happen to Andrew's blood glucose concentration if he ate a meal containing a lot of sugar.

_____ [2 marks]

b Explain your answer to part **a**.

_____ [1 mark]

c Andrew injects himself with insulin each day. What else can he do to control the concentration of glucose in his blood?

_____ [1 mark]

D–C

3 In 1922, F. G. Banting and C. H. Best published a research paper in which they described experiments that they had done on dogs that had had their pancreases removed. They were testing their hypothesis that the pancreas produced something that reduced blood glucose concentration. This is a summary of one of their experiments.

Time	Treatment	Blood glucose concentration	Other results
10.30 am	None	0.35%	
11.00 am	Injection of glucose given	0.40%	Glucose was excreted in the urine for the next four hours
3.00 pm	Injection of pancreas extract given	Rapidly fell to 0.09%	

a Explain why the dog's blood glucose concentration rose to 0.40% at 11.00 am.

_____ [2 marks]

b Explain why glucose was excreted in the dog's urine between 11.00 am and 3.00 pm.

_____ [2 marks]

c Did Banting's and Best's results support their hypothesis? Explain your answer.

_____ [2 marks]

D–C

Cell division – mitosis

1 This cell contains one pair of chromosomes.

  a The cell divides by mitosis. Complete the diagrams to show the chromosomes in the two daughter (new) cells produced after the cell has completed its division.

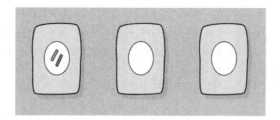

[2 marks]

  b Choose the best word to complete this sentence.

  The new cells that are produced by mitosis are _____ identical to the parent cell.

[1 mark]

2 a Humans have two sets of 23 chromosomes. How many copies of each gene are there in a skin cell?

  _____

[1 mark]

  b Name the kind of cell division that takes place in a skin cell in order to heal a cut.

  _____

[1 mark]

  c Cell division is usually controlled by certain genes. Ultraviolet light can damage these genes in skin cells. Explain what could happen as a result.

  _____

  _____

[2 marks]

Gametes and fertilisation

3 Sperm cells and egg cells are gametes.

  a Explain why gametes must have only 23 chromosomes each.

  _____

[1 mark]

  b i Name the type of division that is used when a cell divides to form gametes.

  _____

[1 mark]

  ii Outline what happens when a cell divides in this way.

  _____

  _____

  _____

[3 marks]

4 a Explain the meaning of the term **allele**.

  _____

[1 mark]

  b Explain how alleles can cause variation in the characteristics of offspring that are produced by sexual reproduction.

  _____

  _____

[3 marks]

Stem cells

1 a Explain the meaning of these words.

    i Stem cell

_____ [1 mark]

    ii Differentiation

_____ [1 mark]

b Stem cells can be obtained from very early human embryos. They are able to divide to form every kind of cell in the body.

    i Explain how embryo stem cells differ from the stem cells found in adult bone marrow.

_____

_____ [2 marks]

    ii Describe how the use of embryo stem cells might be able to treat conditions such as paralysis after the spinal cord has been damaged.

_____

_____ [2 marks]

D–C

2 Parkinson's disease is a condition in which some of the cells in the brain die. These cells are specialised to make a substance called dopamine. Lack of dopamine causes symptoms such as loss of control over movement.

Suggest how stem cells could one day be used to treat Parkinson's disease.

_____

_____ [2 marks]

B–A*

Chromosomes, genes and DNA

3 This diagram shows a cell, and some of the contents of its nucleus.

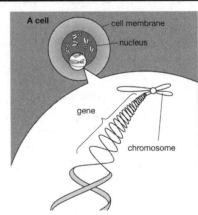

D–C

a Name the chemical that chromosomes are made of.

_____ [1 mark]

b Each chromosome contains many genes. Describe how genes control the function of a cell.

_____ [1 mark]

B–A*

c The functions of many different human genes are now known, and it is possible to find out which varieties of these genes a person has in their cells.

    i Suggest **one** advantage of this.

_____ [1 mark]

    ii Suggest **one** disadvantage.

_____ [1 mark]

Inheritance

1 In pea plants, height is controlled by a single gene. The gene has two alleles, **T** and **t**.
A plant with genes **T** and **t** is tall.

a Which allele is dominant? Explain your answer.

_____

_____ [2 marks]

b Write down the alleles that a short plant has.

_____ [1 mark]

2 In dalmatian dogs, the allele for black spots, B, is dominant to the allele b for brown spots.

a What are the alleles of a homozygous black dog?_____ [1 mark]

b What colour spots does a homozygous recessive dog have?_____ [1 mark]

c What alleles are contained in each sperm of a brown-spotted dog?_____ [1 mark]

d Construct a genetic diagram to show the puppies you would expect to get if a female, homozygous dog with black spots was crossed with a male dog with brown spots.

[3 marks]

How sex is inherited

3 Which determines a child's sex – its mother's egg, or its father's sperm? Explain your answer.

_____

_____

_____ [3 marks]

4 This diagram shows the chromosomes in a person's cells.

a Is the person male or female? Explain your answer.

_____

_____

_____

_____

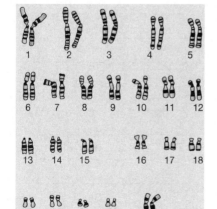

[2 marks]

Inherited disorders

1 Huntington's disease is a disorder of the nervous system. A person with only one allele for Huntington's disease has this disorder.

Explain why it is not possible for a child to inherit Huntington's disease unless one of her parents has this disorder.

_____

_____

_____ [3 marks]

D–C

2 Angela and Sam have two children. Their son has cystic fibrosis. Neither Angela nor Sam has cystic fibrosis and their daughter does not have it either.

a Using the symbols F and f for the alleles, draw a genetic diagram to explain how Angela and Sam had a son with cystic fibrosis, even though they do not have it themselves.

[4 marks]

b When their daughter grows up, could she have a child with cystic fibrosis? Explain your answer.

_____

_____

_____ [3 marks]

B–A*

DNA fingerprinting

3 A mother wants to know which of two possible men is her child's father. DNA fingerprints are made of the mother, child and the two men. Their DNA fingerprints are shown in the diagram.

Which man is the child's father? Explain how you worked it out.

_____

_____

_____

_____

_____

_____

_____

_____

_____

[4 marks]

D–C

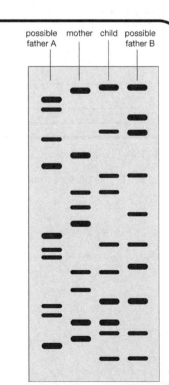

possible father A   mother   child   possible father B

B2b revision checklist

I know:

what enzymes are and what their functions are

☐ enzymes are proteins that act as biological catalysts, speeding up chemical reactions

☐ each enzyme works at an optimum temperature and pH

☐ high temperatures or extremes of pH denature enzymes by affecting the shape of their active sites

☐ they are involved in respiration, photosynthesis, protein synthesis and digestion

☐ enzymes are used in washing powders and in industry

how our bodies keep internal conditions constant

☐ blood sugar levels are controlled by the pancreas, which makes insulin to bring down blood sugar levels

☐ waste products, e.g. carbon dioxide and urea, must be removed from the body

☐ sweating cools the body down and helps to maintain a steady body temperature

☐ if core body temperature is too high, blood vessels supplying the skin capillaries dilate so more blood flows through capillaries and more heat is lost

☐ if core body temperature is too low, blood vessels supplying the skin capillaries constrict to reduce the flow of blood through capillaries; muscles may shiver

some human characteristics show a simple pattern of inheritance

☐ some inherited characteristics are controlled by a single gene

☐ different forms of a gene are called alleles; in homozygous individuals the alleles are the same, in heterozygous individuals they are different

☐ how to construct/interpret a genetic diagram; and how to predict/explain the outcome of crosses between individuals for each possible combination of dominant and recessive alleles of the same gene

☐ in mitosis each new cell has the same number of identical chromosomes as the original

☐ sex chromosomes determine the sex of the offspring (male XY, female XX)

☐ stem cells can specialise into many types of cells

Atomic structure 2

1 Lithium is a metal in Group 1 of the periodic table.

7	**Li**
3	lithium

D–C

a Describe the structure of a lithium nucleus.

_____

_____

[2 marks]

b Three reactions that result in changes to the atom are shown in the table.
Complete the table by filling in the missing information.

B–A*

Type of reaction	Ionisation	Nuclear fission	Nuclear fusion
Change in mass of nucleus (increases/decreases/ stays the same)			
Change to the atom	Loss or gain of electrons		Two nuclei join together

[5 marks]

Electronic structure

2 The table shows some information about how electrons are arranged in a sodium atom.

D–C

a Complete the table to show the same information for magnesium and fluorine.

Periodic table element	23 **Na** 11 sodium	24 **Mg** 12 magnesium	19 **F** 9 fluorine
Number of electrons	11	12	
Electron arrangement	Na	Mg	F
Notation	2, 8, 1		

[5 marks]

b Sodium loses an electron to form a stable ion. What is the electronic structure of a sodium ion?

_____

[1 mark]

3 The following compounds occur naturally in calcite and dolomite ore.

D–C

$CaCO_3$ | $CaMg(CO_3)_2$
compound in calcite ore | **compound in dolomite ore**

a What is the name of each compound?

Compound in calcite _____

Compound in dolomite _____ [2 marks]

b Explain how the compound in dolomite ore forms.

_____

_____

[2 marks]

Mass number and isotopes

1 This question is about the periodic table.

D–C

a Lithium and sodium are both in Group 1 of the periodic table. Give **one similarity** and **one difference** between the electronic configurations of atoms of lithium and sodium.

Similarity _____

Difference _____ [2 marks]

B–A*

b Chlorine has a mass number of 35.5. Explain why the mass number of chlorine is not a whole number.

_____

_____

_____ [3 marks]

Ionic bonding

D–C

2 The diagram shows what happens when a calcium atom reacts with chlorine atoms.

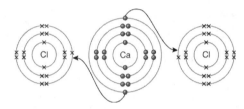

a What is the symbol for the calcium ion that forms? Draw a ring around the **correct** answer.

Ca   **Ca⁺**   **Ca²⁺**   **Ca⁻**   **Ca²⁻** [1 mark]

b What is the formula for calcium chloride?

Formula _____ [1 mark]

D–C

3 Car batteries contain a solution of an ionically bonded compound dissolved in water. The solution conducts electricity.

a Describe how ionic compounds conduct electricity when they are dissolved in water.

_____

_____ [2 marks]

b If a car battery was filled with pure water, the battery would not work. Explain why.

_____

_____ [2 marks]

Ionic compounds

1 The diagram shows how the ions in sodium chloride are arranged when it is molten.

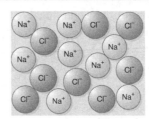

D–C

a Use the diagram to explain why sodium chloride conducts electricity when it is molten.

_____

_____ [2 marks]

b Give **one** reason why sodium chloride cannot conduct electricity when it is a solid.

_____ [1 mark]

2 The diagram shows how electricity can be used to plate silver onto jewellery.

B–A*

a Put a cross on the diagram to show where ions **gain** electrons.

b During this process, silver atoms (**Ag**) lose electrons to form silver ions (**Ag⁺**)

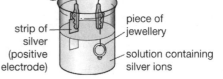

power pack

strip of silver (positive electrode)

piece of jewellery

solution containing silver ions

Explain what happens to a silver atom when it forms a silver ion.

_____

_____ [2 marks]

Covalent bonding

3 Look at the diagrams to show the bonding in chlorine and oxygen. Only the outer shell electrons are shown.

D–C

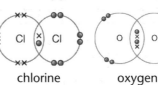

chlorine   oxygen

a The bond between the chlorine atoms is a **single** bond. What type of bond joins the oxygen atoms together?

_____ [1 mark]

b Explain how you can tell.

_____ [1 mark]

c Explain why the oxygen atoms are **not** joined together by a single bond.

_____

_____ [2 marks]

d The two chlorine atoms in each chlorine molecule are very difficult to break apart yet chlorine is a gas at room temperature. Use this information to explain the difference between **bonds** and **intermolecular forces**.

B–A*

_____

_____ [2 marks]

Simple molecules

1 Perfumes are made by dissolving fragrant oils in a solvent. The table shows some information about possible solvents to use in a new perfume.

Name of solvent	Methoxyethane	Ethanol	Water	Naphthol
Solubility of fragrant oil in the solvent	Very soluble	Soluble	Not soluble	Very soluble
Boiling point of solvent	7 °C	78 °C	100 °C	295 °C

a Which of the solvents has the strongest intermolecular forces?

Name of solvent _____

Explain your reasoning.

_____ [1 mark]

b Complete the sentences about the solvents.
  i Methoxyethane is not a suitable solvent to make perfume because

_____ [1 mark]

  ii Ethanol is the best solvent for making perfume because _____

_____ [1 mark]

  iii Naphthol is not a suitable solvent to make perfume because _____

_____ [1 mark]

c Suggest one **other** property that needs to be tested to check that the solvents are suitable to use to make perfumes.

_____ [1 mark]

Giant covalent structures

2 Diamond and graphite are both macromolecules that contain carbon atoms.

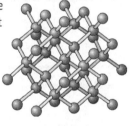

diamond

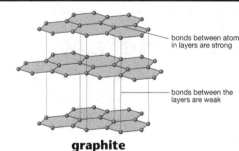

bonds between atoms in layers are strong

bonds between the layers are weak

graphite

a Compare the diagram of graphite to the diagram of diamond.
Explain why graphite is soft and slippery but diamond is not.

_____

_____

_____ [3 marks]

b Graphite is used to strengthen polymers to use to build aeroplanes. One reason that graphite can be used in this way is because it is lightweight and has a low density. Use the structure of graphite to suggest why graphite has a low density.

_____ [1 mark]

c The bonds between the layers are formed by delocalised electrons. What does the word **delocalised** mean?

_____ [1 mark]

Metals

1 The diagram shows the structure of a metal.

a Label the diagram. [2 marks]

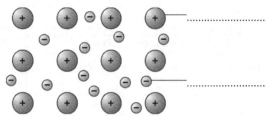

....

....

b Use the diagram to help you to explain what happens when a metal conducts electricity.

_____ [1 mark]

D–C

2 Read the article about mercury.

B–A*

> **MERCURY**
> Mercury used to be called 'quicksilver' because it is a liquid at room temperature. Liquid mercury forms small drops that change shape and flow quickly over surfaces. Like other metals, mercury transfers both electrical and thermal energy due the delocalised electrons in its structure.

a Explain what happens to the structure of mercury when it changes shape.

_____ [1 mark]

b The article states that mercury 'transfers both electrical and thermal energy'.
   i Explain what this statement means.

_____

_____ [2 marks]

   ii How do the delocalised electrons help the transfer of energy through metals?

_____ [1 mark]

Alkali metals

3 The diagrams show the electron arrangements in some atoms.

B–A*

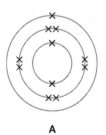

| A | B | C |

a All the atoms are metals. Explain how the electron arrangements show this.

_____ [1 mark]

b Which atom is of a metal from Group 1? _____

   Explain how you can tell. _____ [2 marks]

c Which atom has the highest number of protons in its nucleus? _____

   Explain how you can tell. _____ [2 marks]

Halogens

D–C

1 The diagram shows the electron arrangement in a fluorine atom.

fluorine atom   **fluoride ion**

   a Complete the second diagram to show the electron arrangement in a fluoride **ion**.   [1 mark]

   b What is the charge on a fluoride ion?

        _____   [1 mark]

   c Which of the following elements will react with fluorine gas to produce fluoride ions? Draw a ring around the **correct** answer.

      chlorine   **oxygen**   **sodium**   **helium**   [1 mark]

D–C

2 Candice bubbles some fluorine gas through solutions of some compounds of halogens.
Table 1 shows her results.   **Table 2**

Solution of compound	Does it react with fluorine gas?	Colour after reaction
Sodium chloride	Yes	Very pale green
Sodium bromide	Yes	
Sodium iodide	Yes	

Solution of compound	Does it react with bromine?
Sodium fluoride	
Sodium chloride	
Sodium iodide	

   a **i** Complete **Table 1** by filling in the missing colours.   [2 marks]

       ii Give the names of the two products of the reaction between fluorine and sodium chloride.

        _____   [1 mark]

   b Candice carries out a similar experiment. This time she adds bromine instead of fluorine to three halogen compounds. Complete **Table 2** to show whether or not a reaction will happen in each case.   [2 marks]

Nanoparticles

B–A*

3 Nanoparticles can be used to carry molecules of drugs into the human body. At the moment such treatments are expensive but in the future they may become routine.

   a What does the term **nanoparticle** mean?

      _____

      _____   [2 marks]

   b Explain how the structure of nanoparticles enables them to carry other molecules.

      _____

      _____   [2 marks]

   c Companies paid millions of pounds for the research that was needed to develop nanoparticles. Explain how those companies benefit now that nanoparticles have been developed.

      _____

      _____

      _____   [3 marks]

Smart materials

1 Smart materials have a wide range of uses.

A, **B**, **C** and **D**, are different types of smart materials:

A shape changing alloy   **B** photochromic polymer
C thermochromic material   **D** electroluminescent material

What type of smart material is used for each of the following uses?

Spectacle frame made from smart material type _____

Dials in a car light up when a current passes
through them. They contain smart material type _____

The plastic visor goes dark when it is very sunny.
It is made from smart material type _____

The pictures on this mug change when it is filled with a hot drink.
It is coated with smart material type

_____

[4 marks]

Compounds

2 The table shows some information about hydrogen, oxygen and water.

Name	Hydrogen	Oxygen	Water
Formula	H_2	O_2	H_2O
Properties	Very flammable gas	Very reactive gas	Unreactive liquid

a Explain why hydrogen is an **element** but water is a **compound**.

_____

[2 marks]

b A mixture of hydrogen and oxygen react together explosively when they are lit. The product is water. Explain the differences between a **mixture** and a **compound** using this information.

_____

_____

_____

[3 marks]

c When hydrogen reacts with oxygen, the volume of hydrogen used up is always twice the volume of oxygen that is used up. Use ideas about the formula of water to explain why.

_____

_____

[2 marks]

3 Complete these equations.

a N_2 +   _____ H_2 →   _____ NH_3

b   Mg   +   _____ HNO_3 → $Mg(NO_3)_2$ +   _____

[4 marks]

Percentage composition

1 Harvey works out the percentage of elements in some compounds. He tests the following compounds:

$$O_2 \qquad CO \qquad CO_2 \qquad O_3 \qquad CH_4$$

Here are his results.

> Percentage of oxygen in compound A = 57%
> Percentage of oxygen in compound B = 72%

a Which of the compounds that Harvey tests are most likely to be compound A and compound B?

Compound A _____ Compound B _____ [2 marks]

b Explain your reasoning.

_____ [1 mark]

Moles

2 Sulfur dioxide is a pollutant gas that comes from power stations. It is made when sulfur impurities in fuel burn. Some people are protesting against the amount of sulfur dioxide coming from a power station.

Sulfur in fuel produces twice the amount of sulfur dioxide when it burns.

a Laura does some calculations to check to see if the sign is true. Complete her calculations by filling in the spaces.
(atomic mass of sulfur, S: 32; atomic mass of oxygen, O: 16)

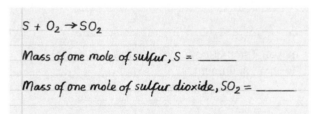

$S + O_2 \rightarrow SO_2$

Mass of one mole of sulfur, S = _____

Mass of one mole of sulfur dioxide, SO_2 = _____

[2 marks]

b Laura calculates the percentage mass of sulfur in sulfur dioxide. Complete her calculation.

> Atomic mass of sulfur, S = 32
>
> Atomic mass of oxygen, O = 16
>
> Percentage mass of sulfur in SO_2 =
>
> _____ %

_____

_____ [2 marks]

c A power station burns 80 tonnes of coal each day. Eighty tonnes of coal contains 320 kg of sulfur. What mass of sulfur dioxide will 320 kg of sulfur produce when it burns?

_____

_____ [2 marks]

Yield of product

1 Harry works in a factory that makes a chemical compound that is added to painkiller tablets.

> Our method for making this compound has a very high yield. This is important because it makes the process more profitable for the company. We work to make our actual yield as near as possible to our theoretical yield so that we have a high atom economy for the process.

a Give **two** reasons why having a high yield makes the process more profitable.

_____

_____

_____ [2 marks]

b What does Harry mean when he says the process has a high **atom economy**?

_____

_____ [2 marks]

c Explain the difference between **theoretical** and **actual** yield.

_____

_____ [2 marks]

D–C

B–A*

---

2 Rose makes some magnesium oxide by burning magnesium in air. She writes an equation for the reaction.

$$Mg + \tfrac{1}{2}O_2 \rightarrow MgO$$

a Eve uses 2.4 g of magnesium. Calculate the theoretical yield of magnesium oxide from 2.4 g of magnesium.
(relative atomic mass, Mg: 24; relative atomic mass, O: 16)

_____

_____

_____ [3 marks]

b Rose weighs the magnesium oxide she makes. The magnesium oxide has a mass of 3.0 g. Calculate the percentage yield for the experiment.

_____

_____ [2 marks]

D–C

Reversible reactions

3 Ethanol (C_2H_5OH) is a solvent used to make perfumes. It can be made by reacting ethene gas (C_2H_4) with water. The reaction is reversible.

a Write the equation for the reaction. Include the sign to show that the reaction is reversible.

_____ [1 mark]

b Use the substances in the equation to answer these questions.
   i Give the fomula of **one** substance from the equation that has the **same** empirical formula and molecular formula.

_____ [1 mark]

   ii Give the fomula of **one** substance from the equation that has a **different** empirical formula and molecular formula.

_____ [1 mark]

D–C

Equilibrium 1

1 Ethanol is made on an industrial scale by reacting ethene gas with water vapour in a reactor.

ethene + water vapour $\rightleftharpoons$ ethanol

Conditions
High temperature: 300 °C
High pressure: 70 atm
Catalyst: phosphoric acid

a Which of the reaction conditions will change the rate of reaction?

A all of them

B only temperature

C temperature and pressure

D only the catalyst [1 mark]

b When the gases come out of the reactor the ethanol is separated out. The rest of the gases are recycled back into the reactor again. Explain why this is necessary.

_____

_____ [2 marks]

c Complete the table to show what effect a change in each of the reaction conditions would make to the yield.

Change to reaction condition	**Effect on yield (increases/ decreases/stays the same)**
A higher temperature	
A higher pressure	
Using less catalyst	

[3 marks]

Haber process

2 The diagram shows a plan of the Haber process for making ammonia.

$$N_2 + 3H_2 \rightleftharpoons 2NH_3$$

GASES IN
1 _____
and
2 _____

REACTOR

recycled gas

beds of
3 _____
catalyst

OUT
4 _____

a Complete the diagram by adding the missing labels.

[3 marks]

b A pressure of 200 atmospheres is used for the process.
   i Give **two** advantages of running the process at a high pressure.

_____

_____ [2 marks]

   ii Give **one** reason why it is not practical to run the process at even higher pressures.

_____ [1 mark]

c The reaction to make ammonia is an equilibrium reaction. Gases from the end of the process are recycled back to the start. Explain why this is necessary.

_____

_____ [2 marks]

C2a revision checklist

I know:

how sub-atomic particles help us to understand the structure of substances

☐ an element's mass number is the number of protons plus the number of neutrons in an atom

☐ an element's atomic number is the number of protons in an atom

☐ electrons arranged in shells around the nucleus have different energy levels and this can be used to explain what happens when elements react and how atoms join together to form different types of substances

☐ how to write balanced chemical equations for reactions

☐ metals consist of giant structures of atoms arranged in a regular pattern, with delocalised electrons

how structures influence the properties and uses of substances

☐ ionic bonding is the attraction between oppositely charged ions

☐ ionic compounds are giant lattice structures with high melting points that conduct electricity when molten or dissolved

☐ non-metal atoms can share pairs of electrons to form covalent bonds

☐ giant covalent structures are macromolecules that are hard, have high melting points but do not conduct electricity

☐ simple molecular elements (e.g. oxygen) and compounds (water) have weak intermolecular forces

☐ delocalised electrons in metals and graphite enable them to conduct heat and electricity as they are free to move through the whole structure

☐ nanoparticles are very small structures with special properties because of their unique atom arrangement

how much can we make and how much we need to use

☐ the relative masses of atoms can be used to calculate how much to react and how much we can produce, because no atoms are gained or lost in chemical reactions

☐ the percentage of an element in a compound can be calculated from the relative masses of the element in the formula and the relative formula mass of the compound

☐ how to calculate chemical quantities involving empirical formulae, reacting masses and percentage yield and how to balance symbol equations

☐ high atom economy (atom utilisation) is important for sustainable development and economic reasons

☐ reversible reactions carried out in a 'closed' system will eventually reach equilibrium

Rates of reactions

1 Salma reacts magnesium ribbon with an acid. She uses a gas syringe to measure the volume of gas that is given off after 50 seconds.

a Draw a fully labelled diagram to show how Salma sets up her experiment.

[3 marks]

b Salma carries out her experiment three times with three different concentrations of acid. Here are her results.

Acid	Volume of gas given off in 50 s	Rate of reaction (cm³ of gas per second)
Concentration A	40	0.8
Concentration B	160	3.2
Concentration C	90	

i Calculate the rate of reaction for the acid with concentration C.

_____

_____ [2 marks]

ii Which acid is the most concentrated? Explain your reasoning.

_____

_____ [2 marks]

c Salma keeps a record of the concentrations of acid she uses. She knows that she needs to control all factors to make sure her results can be repeated. List **three other** factors that Salma needs to control.

1_____ 2_____ 3_____ [3 marks]

Following the rate of reaction

2 Callum is investigating the rate of reaction of marble chips with acid. He knows that the reaction produces carbon dioxide gas. He set up this experiment to find out the rate of reaction.

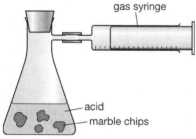

gas syringe

acid

marble chips

a What **two** measurements will Callum need to make to follow the rate of reaction?

1 _____

2 _____ [2 marks]

b How will Callum be able to tell when the reaction has stopped?

_____ [1 mark]

c What **other** change could Callum measure to follow the rate of reaction? Draw a ring around the **correct** answer.

colour   **mass**   **volume of acid**   **size of chips**   [1 mark]

Collision theory

1 The diagram in **box A** shows acid particles reacting
with a large lump of zinc.

a How would the diagram change if
  i the acid was more concentrated?

_____

_____

[1 mark]

  ii the temperature was increased?

_____

[1 mark]

b When zinc powder is used instead of lumps of zinc the reaction is faster.
Use ideas about particle collisions to explain why.

_____

_____

[2 marks]

D–C

acid
particle

zinc

Box A

2 Gases behave very differently in the ozone layer. Air at the surface is at a much higher
pressure than gases in the ozone layer. Some parts of the ozone layer are very hot.
These conditions alter the concentrations of gases.

B–A*

a What happens to the concentration of a gas if its **temperature** is increased?
Explain your reasoning.

_____

_____

[2 marks]

b What happens to the concentration of a gas if its **pressure** is increased?
Explain your reasoning.

_____

_____

[2 marks]

Heating things up

3 Carbon dioxide is made when copper carbonate reacts
with hydrochloric acid. David investigates the reaction.
The diagram shows how he set up his experiment.

D–C

a What would you expect to happen to the mass of
the flask during the experiment?
Explain your reasoning.

_____

_____

_____

_____

[3 marks]

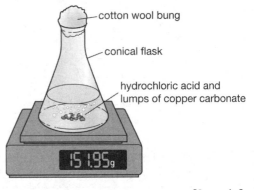

cotton wool bung

conical flask

hydrochloric acid and
lumps of copper carbonate

151.95g

b David carries out his experiment at different temperatures. He calculates that the
rate of reaction doubles with each 10 °C rise in temperature. Use ideas about
collisions and energy to explain why this happens.

B–A*

_____

_____

[3 marks]

Grind it up, speed it up

D–C

1 Isabel carries out some experiments. She reacts zinc with acid in a flask. She uses different conditions. The table shows the conditions she uses.

Experiment	A	B	C	D
Size of zinc lumps	Large lumps	Small lumps	Large lumps	Small lumps
Concentration of acid	Low	High	High	Low
Temperature	20 °C	50 °C	50 °C	20 °C

a Explain why the zinc pieces dissolve fastest in experiment B.

_____

_____ [3 marks]

B–A*

b In experiment A, hydrogen was produced at a rate of 4.5 cm^3/s.
  i Suggest a value for the rate of reaction in experiment D. Explain your reasoning.

Rate _____

Reason _____ [3 marks]

  ii Suggest a value for the rate of reaction in experiment B. Explain your reasoning.

Rate _____

Reason _____ [3 marks]

Concentrate now

D–C

2 Leo does an experiment (experiment 1). He reacts some acid with some marble chips. He measures the change in mass as the reaction happens. He stops measuring when no more carbon dioxide is given off. Leo repeats the experiment. He uses the same amount of acid and marble chips, but this time he adds some water to the flask (experiment 2).

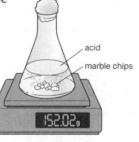

acid
marble chips

152.02 g

at the start

151.95 g

at the end

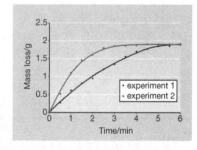

a What has been used up when the reaction stops? _____ [2 marks]

b The reactions for both experiments were fast at the beginning and then slowed down. Explain why.

_____

_____ [3 marks]

c Explain why the graphs for experiment 1 and experiment 2 are different shapes.

_____ [2 marks]

d In each experiment, Leo uses 25 cm^3 of 2 mol/dm^3 hydrochloric acid.
  i What volume of water would Leo need to add to the acid so that the reaction rate was exactly half as fast? _____

  ii Explain your reasoning. _____

_____ [2 marks]

Catalysts

1 Hydrogen peroxide (H_2O_2) is used to bleach hair. It slowly decomposes to form water and oxygen gas.

a Complete the equation for this reaction.

$2H_2O_2 \rightarrow$ _____   [2 marks]

b Sophie did some experiments using hydrogen peroxide.
In experiment 1 she used hydrogen peroxide with no catalyst.
In experiment 2 she added 0.2 g of manganese dioxide catalyst.

The diagram shows the activation energy for experiment 1. Draw and label a
second curve on the diagram to show the activation energy for experiment 2.

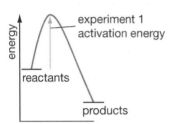

[2 marks]

c Sophie filtered off the manganese dioxide at the end of experiment 3 and
dried it thoroughly before weighing it. What mass of manganese dioxide
should Sophie have? Explain your reasoning.

Mass _____

Reason _____   [2 marks]

D–C

B–A*

2 The Haber process is used to make ammonia for making fertilisers. Iron is used as
catalyst in the reaction.

a The iron catalyst is packed into the reaction tower. It is only replaced about every 15 years.
Why does the iron catalyst have such a long lifetime?

_____   [1 mark]

b Many metal catalysts are very expensive. Give **two** reasons why they make
industrial processes cheaper in the long run.

1 _____

2 _____   [2 marks]

D–C

Energy changes

3 a The table shows some information about temperature and energy changes during three reactions.
Complete the table by filling in the boxes.

Reaction	Temperature change	Exothermic or endothermic?
Dissolving ammonium nitrate in water	Decreases	
Adding zinc powder to copper		Exothermic
Adding magnesium ribbon to an acid	Increases	

[2 marks]

b Which of these reactions is likely to be exothermic? Draw a ring around the **two correct** answers.

oxidation   **thermal decomposition**   **neutralisation**   **evaporation**   [2 marks]

D–C

Equilibrium 2

1 Hydrogen for making ammonia can be made by reacting methane gas with steam. The reaction is reversible.

$$CH_4 \quad + \quad H_2O \quad \underset{\text{exothermic}}{\overset{\text{endothermic}}{\rightleftharpoons}} \quad CO \quad + \quad 3H_2$$

a What is the name of the other product of the reaction? _____ [1 mark]

b Would a low or a high temperature give the highest yield of hydrogen? Explain your reasoning.

_____

_____ [2 marks]

c In practice, higher temperatures are almost always used for industrial processes. Explain why.

_____ [1 mark]

Industrial processes

2 The flow chart shows how ammonia is made in the Haber process.

a Write a word equation for the reaction that happens in the reactor. Include the sign to show that the reaction is reversible.

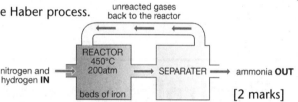

_____ [2 marks]

b i Why does the reactor contain iron?

_____ [2 marks]

ii The iron is in the form of very small pieces rather than large lumps. Explain why.

_____ [2 marks]

c The unreacted gases travel back to the reactor through a pipe.
i Name the **two** gases that travel through the pipe.

_____ and _____ [1 mark]

ii Give a reason why this reaction never gives 100% yield.

_____ [1 mark]

3 The table shows some data about the yield of ammonia from the Haber process under different conditions.

Temperature (°C)	Pressure (atm)	Yield
400	200	40%
400	100	25%
500	100	15%

a Predict the yield of ammonia at 400 °C and 50 atm pressure.

_____ % [1 mark]

b In industry, the optimum conditions for the Haber process are 450 °C and 200 atm pressure.
i Explain why this temperature is better to use than either a lower or a higher temperature.

_____ [2 marks]

ii Explain why a relatively high pressure is chosen.

_____ [2 marks]

iii Use your answers to explain what the term 'optimum conditions' mean.

_____ [2 marks]

Free ions

1 The diagram shows the arrangement of ions in solid lithium chloride.

a Explain how the structure of lithium chloride is typical of an ionic solid.

_____

_____

_____

[2 marks]

b Solid lithium chloride does not conduct electricity but a solution of lithium chloride dissolved in water is a good conductor. Explain why.

_____

_____

[2 marks]

c When an electric current passes through a solution of lithium chloride, a greenish gas forms.

i What is the name of this gas?

_____

[1 mark]

ii At which electrode does this gas form? Explain your reasoning.

_____

_____

[2 marks]

Electrolysis equations

2 Read the article about the electrolysis of molten sodium chloride.

ELECTROLYIS OF MOLTEN SODIUM CHLORIDE
Sodium chloride is usually electrolysed by passing an electric current through a solution of the salt in water. However, this does not make sodium metal – a gas forms at the negative electrode instead. Electrolysing **molten** sodium chloride is very difficult because it has to be carried out at about 1000 °C. At this temperature, the electricity splits the salt to form sodium metal and chlorine gas.

a i Name the gas that forms at the negative electrode during the electrolysis of aqueous sodium chloride solution.

_____

[1 mark]

ii Explain why this gas forms instead of sodium metal.

_____

[1 mark]

b Why must a high temperature be used for the electrolysis of molten sodium chloride?

_____

_____

[2 marks]

c i Complete the half equation to show what happens to a sodium ion during the electrolysis of molten sodium chloride.

Na^+ ⟶

[2 marks]

ii Explain why this reaction is an example of a **reduction** reaction.

_____

[1 mark]

Uses for electrolysis

1 The diagram shows what happens when sodium chloride is electrolysed. Complete the labels on the diagram to show the names of each product of the electrolysis and give a use of each.

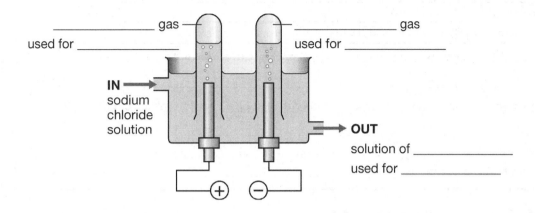

_____ gas

used for _____

_____ gas

used for _____

IN sodium chloride solution

OUT

solution of _____

used for _____

[6 marks]

2 Copper is purified by electrolysis.

a Complete the sentences to explain what happens during the electrolysis.

When copper is purified, both electrodes are

made from _____ .

A block of impure copper is used as

the _____ electrode.

electrode made of pure copper

electrode made of impure copper

solution containing copper ions

Copper ions from the solution form pure copper by _____ two electrons.

[3 marks]

b Complete the equations to show what happens at each electrode.

Positive electrode	Negative electrode
$Cu(s) \rightarrow$	$Cu^{2+}(aq)$

[2 marks]

Acids and metals

3 The table shows the reactivity of some metals.

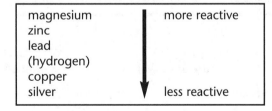

magnesium
zinc
lead
(hydrogen)
copper
silver

more reactive

less reactive

a Holly has samples of zinc and copper metals and some dilute hydrochloric acid. Explain how she uses these substances to show that zinc is more reactive than hydrogen in the reactivity series but copper is less reactive.

_____

_____

_____

[3 marks]

Making salts from bases

1 Karim makes some salts. The table shows what substances he uses.

Substances used	Salt formed
Zinc and dilute hydrochloric acid	
Copper oxide and dilute sulfuric acid	Copper sulfate

D–C

a What is the name of the salt formed when zinc reacts with dilute hydrochloric acid?

_____ [1 mark]

b i Explain why Karim uses copper oxide rather than copper metal to make copper sulfate.

B–A*

_____ [1 mark]

ii Give the name of another copper compound that Karim could add to the
acid to make copper sulfate. _____ [1 mark]

Acids and alkalis

2 Max makes sodium chloride. He puts some sodium hydroxide solution
(an alkali) in a flask and adds hydrochloric acid from a burette. He adds
litmus solution to the sodium hydroxide to act as an indicator. He adds
hydrochloric acid to the sodium hydroxide until he reaches the end point
when all the sodium hydroxide has been neutralised. The table shows the
litmus at different pHs.

D–C

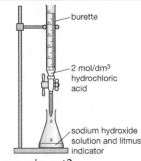

burette

2 mol/dm³
hydrochloric
acid

sodium hydroxide
solution and litmus
indicator

pH below 7	pH above 7
red	blue

a What colour change will the litmus indictor show at the end point of the experiment?

From _____ to _____ [1 mark]

b Why could litmus indicator **not** be used to measure the exact pH of the sodium hydroxide?

_____ [1 mark]

c Max wants to make a pure solution of sodium chloride without an indicator.

i Describe how he can do this.

_____

_____ [3 marks]

ii How can Max make sodium chloride crystals from his solution?

_____ [1 mark]

3 Compounds A, B and C are used in fertilisers.

B–A*

NH_4NO_3	$(NH_4)_2SO_4$	$K(NH_4)_2PO_4$
compound A	**compound B**	**compound C**

a Explain why all three compounds are suitable to use as fertilisers.

_____ [1 mark]

b Name compound A. _____ [1 mark]

c Give the name and fomula of the **acid** that would be needed to make compound B.

_____ [2 marks]

d The three most important elements for plant growth are potassium, nitrogen and
phosphorus. Which compound contains all three elements?

_____ [1 mark]

Neutralisation

1 The table shows some information about the ions in some solutions.

a Complete the table by filling in the empty boxes.
[2 marks]

Solution	Type of positive ion	Type of negative ion
NaOH	Na$^+$	OH$^-$
H$_2$SO$_4$	H$^+$	SO$_4{}^{2-}$
	Na$^+$	SO$_4{}^{2-}$
HBr	H$^+$	

b **i** Which solution in the table is an alkali?

_____ [1 mark]

ii Explain how you can tell.

_____ [1 mark]

2 This question is about how ions react during neutralisation reactions. This equation shows the ions produced by lithium hydroxide when it dissolves in water.

$$LiOH(aq) \longrightarrow Li^+(aq) \ + \ OH^-(aq)$$

a Write a similar equation to show the ions produced by hydrochloric acid, HCl(aq), in water.

_____ [2 marks]

b When lithium hydroxide and hydrochloric acid react together, water is formed by the reaction between hydroxide ions and hydrogen ions.
i Write an ionic equation to show the reaction that happens when water forms.

_____ [1 mark]

ii Explain why this equation is the same for all neutralisation reactions.

_____
_____ [3 marks]

iii Give the name of the salt that forms during the reaction.

_____ [1 mark]

Precipitation

3 Read the article about removing pollutants from water.

> **REMOVING POLLUTANTS FROM WATER**
> Most pollutants can be removed from water by precipitation reactions. Positively charged metal ions are usually removed by reacting them with sodium carbonate or sodium hydroxide. Negative ions containing non-metals can be removed by adding calcium compounds. Once the precipitates are formed, they are easy to remove from the water.

a Give the name of **two** compounds that form when lead ions are removed from the water.

_____ [1 mark]

b Give the name of the compound that forms when phosphate ions are removed from the water.

_____ [1 mark]

c Explain why the compounds that form are easily removed from the water.

_____
_____ [2 marks]

C2b revision checklist

I know:

how we can control the rates of chemical reactions

☐ the rate of a reaction can be found by measuring the amount of a reactant used or the amount of product formed over time

☐ reactions can be speeded up by increasing the: temperature; concentration of a solution; pressure of a gas; surface area of a solid; and by using a catalyst

☐ particles must collide with sufficient energy in order to react; the minimum energy required is the activation energy

☐ concentrations of solutions are given in moles per cubic decimetre (mol/dm^3); equal volumes of solutions of the same molar concentration contain the same number of particles of solute

☐ equal volumes of gases contain the same number of molecules

whether chemical reactions always release energy

☐ chemical reactions involve energy transfers

☐ exothermic reactions give OUT energy; endothermic reactions take IN energy

☐ in reversible reactions, equilibrium is reached at a point when the rate of the reverse reaction balances the rate of the forward reaction

☐ the relative amounts of all the reacting substances at equilibrium depend on the conditions of the reaction; this principle is used to determine the optimum conditions for the Haber process

how can we use ions in solutions

☐ when molten or dissolved in water, ions in ionic compounds are free to move

☐ passing an electric current through an ionic compound breaks it down into its elements: this is called electrolysis

☐ at the negative electrode, positively charged ions gain electrons (reduction) and at the positive electrode, negatively charged ions lose electrons (oxidation)

☐ electrolysis of sodium chloride solution makes hydrogen, chlorine and sodium hydroxide

☐ how to complete and balance supplied half equations for the reactions occurring at the electrodes during electrolysis.

☐ metal oxides and hydroxides are bases and react with acids to form salts

☐ soluble salts can be made from reacting an acid with a metal or a base and insoluble salts can be made by mixing solutions of ions

☐ in neutralisation reactions, H^+ ions from acids react with OH^- ions to produce water

See how it moves!

D–C

1 The distance-time graph shows the motion of a bus.

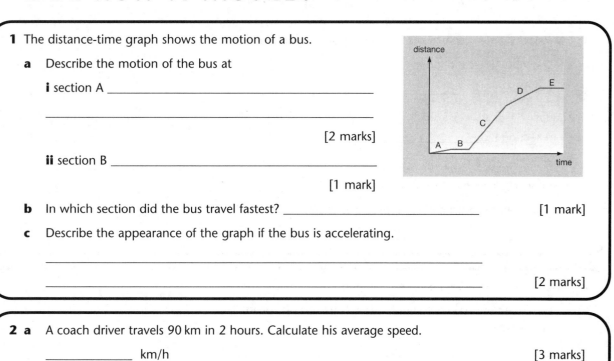

  a Describe the motion of the bus at

    i section A _____

    _____

      [2 marks]

    ii section B _____

      [1 mark]

  b In which section did the bus travel fastest? _____ [1 mark]

B–A*

  c Describe the appearance of the graph if the bus is accelerating.

    _____

    _____

      [2 marks]

D–C

2 a A coach driver travels 90 km in 2 hours. Calculate his average speed.

    _____ km/h   [3 marks]

  b Explain why the coach does not always travel at this average speed.

    _____

    _____

      [2 marks]

Speed isn't everything

D–C

3 a What is velocity?

    _____ [2 marks]

B–A*

  b Describe the velocity of a bung on a piece of string as Imran swings it around his head.

    _____

    _____ [2 marks]

  c What force stops the bung flying off in a straight line?

    _____ [1 mark]

D–C

4 The diagram shows Simon firing an arrow.

  a What is the speed of the arrow just before it leaves the bow?

    _____ m/s

      [1 mark]

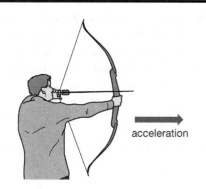

acceleration

  b After 0.5 s, the arrow reaches its top speed of 150 m/s. Calculate the acceleration of the arrow.

    _____ m/s^2

      [3 marks]

Velocity-time graphs

1 The velocity-time graph shows the motion of Alice on her bicycle.

a Describe Alice's motion at

i section A _____

[1 mark]

ii section B _____

[1 mark]

b In which section is Alice travelling slowest? _____ [1 mark]

c How could you tell if Alice stopped moving?

_____ [1 mark]

2 The diagram shows the distance-time graph for a cyclist.

a Describe how you could use the graph to find his speed at any time.

_____

_____

_____

[2 marks]

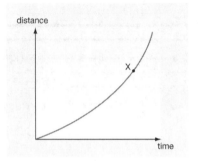

b Explain how you could find the total distance travelled at any time from the graph.

_____ [1 mark]

Let's force it!

3 a The diagram shows the forces acting on a car moving forwards.

i What is the size of the resultant force?

_____

[1 mark]

backward force = 400N   forward force = 800N

ii Describe the motion of the car including its direction.

_____

_____ [2 marks]

b The driver reduces the force from the engine until is the same size as air resistance. Complete the sentence by choosing the correct word from the box.

balanced	unbalanced	constant	changing

The forces are _____ . [1 mark]

c Describe the motion of the car now. _____

_____ [2 marks]

d Describe how you could find the resultant force if the forces act in different directions.

_____

_____ [3 marks]

Force and acceleration

1 a Pete is pushing a shopping trolley. He puts more shopping in.
What happens to the force needed to make the trolley move faster?

_____

[1 mark]

b The mass of the trolley is 20 kg. What force is needed to make it accelerate
by 4 m/s^2? Include the units in your answer.

_____

_____

_____

[3 marks]

c Describe how the mass of the trolley could be found using a forcemeter and
an accelerometer.

_____

_____

_____

[3 marks]

2 Kamal is investigating the acceleration caused by different forces.   Here is a table of his results.

a Explain whether his results prove that acceleration
is proportional to the force used.

Force	Acceleration
1 N	2 m/s^2
2 N	4 m/s^2
3 N	6 m/s^2
4 N	7 m/s^2
5 N	10 m/s^2

_____

_____

_____

[2 marks]

b Explain which one of his results should be repeated.

_____

_____

[2 marks]

Balanced forces

3 A van is trying to pull another car out of a ditch. They are not moving.
a What can you say about the size of the force from the van and the size of
the force from the car?

_____

[1 mark]

b A tractor is used instead of the van. It pulls the car out. How does the force
from the tractor compare with the force from the car?

_____

[1 mark]

c As the tractor accelerates, so does the car. Explain why this makes the car feel heavier for the
tractor to pull.

_____

_____

[2 marks]

Terminal velocity

1 The cyclist is travelling at a steady speed. Friction is one force that slows him down.

a Describe how the size of this force changes as he travels faster.

_____

[1 mark]

b What is **terminal velocity**?

_____

[1 mark]

c The cyclist starts to pedal harder and accelerates until he reaches a faster terminal velocity. Describe how the forces on him change as his speed changes.

_____

_____

_____

[3 marks]

2 Skydivers open parachutes to help them land safely.

a What force increases when the parachute is open?

_____

[1 mark]

b Explain why this helps the parachutist to slow down.

_____

_____

[2 marks]

c Explain how the shape of the parachute can affect the terminal velocity of a skydiver.

_____

_____

[2 marks]

Stop!

3 a Stopping distance can be split into two parts. What are these called?

_____

_____

[2 marks]

b Nicole is taking her first driving lesson. Why will her thinking distance be longer than her driving instructor's?

_____

[1 mark]

c On her second lesson, Nicole was very tired. How will this affect her stopping distance?

_____

_____

[2 marks]

d Nicole's car has been fitted with new tyres. Explain how these will help to reduce her stopping distance.

_____

_____

[3 marks]

Moving through fluids

D–C

1 Charlotte is comparing the speed that a marble falls through different liquids.

a First she drops the marble in a cylinder of water. Explain why it reaches its terminal velocity.

_____

_____ [2 marks]

b Next, she drops the marble through thick honey in the same sized cylinder. Explain why the terminal velocity will change.

_____

_____ [2 marks]

B–A*

c Explain why the density of the honey affects the terminal velocity of the marble.

_____ [1 mark]

Energy to move

D–C

2 a Complete the sentences.

A hairdryer is designed to transfer electrical energy as _____

energy to _____ energy. [2 marks]

b What is the main energy change in a light bulb?

_____ to _____ [2 marks]

D–C

3 Greg is driving his electric car. The batteries ran out and the car stopped.

a Explain what has happened to the energy from the battery.

_____

_____ [2 marks]

b Why did the batteries run out more quickly when he drove the car on a rough surface?

_____

_____ [2 marks]

B–A*

c Some electric vehicles could use flywheels to increase the efficiency of their batteries. Explain why a flywheel could help reduce energy losses caused when a vehicle brakes.

_____

_____ [2 marks]

Working hard

1 Muhammed did 12 J of work when he lifted an apple.

a How much energy was transferred to the apple?

_____ J   [1 mark]

b What force was he working against when he lifted up the apple?

_____   [1 mark]

c Muhammed dragged a box of apples 2 metres along the ground. He measured the force needed as 25 N. How much **work** did he do?

_____ J   [3 marks]

d Explain why he did more work on the box when he started dragging the box up a slope.

_____

_____   [2 marks]

D–C

B–A*

How much energy?

2 Complete the spaces in the sentences.

Andrea has a large elastic harness attached to her when she does a bungee jump

from the top of a bridge. As she jumps, the _____ energy she

has on the bridge changes into _____ energy as she falls.

At the bottom of the jump, the rope is fully extended and it gains

_____ energy. Eventually she stops moving because all the

energy has spread as _____ energy to the surroundings.

[4 marks]

D–C

3 Ryan is playing rugby. He runs fast holding the ball, giving the ball kinetic energy.

a Explain what is meant by **kinetic energy**.

_____   [1 mark]

b The ball is kicked upwards. When the ball is at its highest point, what forms of energy does it have?

_____   [2 marks]

c Calculate the kinetic energy the ball has when it travels at 10 m/s. The ball's mass is 0.3 kg.

_____   [3 marks]

D–C

B–A*

116

Momentum

D–C

1 a Complete the sentences:

    i One example of a scalar quantity is _____ .   [1 mark]

    ii One example of a vector quantity is _____ .   [1 mark]

b What is the **momentum** of a ball? Its mass is 0.5 kg and it travels at 8 m/s.

    _____ kg m/s   [3 marks]

D–C

2 The diagram shows two trolleys colliding.

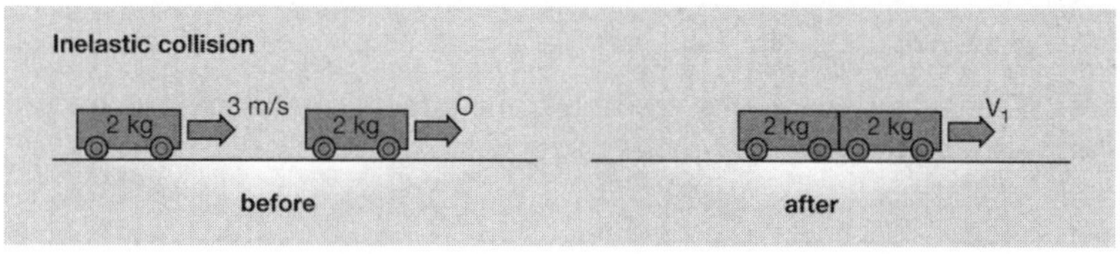

Inelastic collision

before	after
2 kg → 3 m/s 2 kg → O	2 kg 2 kg → V₁

a Calculate the total momentum before the collision.

    _____ kg m/s   [3 marks]

b Write down the total momentum after the collision.

    _____ kg m/s   [1 mark]

c Calculate the speed that the joined-up trolley moves off with.

    _____

    _____   [3 marks]

Off with a bang!

D–C

3 a Jake blows up a balloon but does not tie a knot in it. Describe how the balloon and air move when he lets it go.

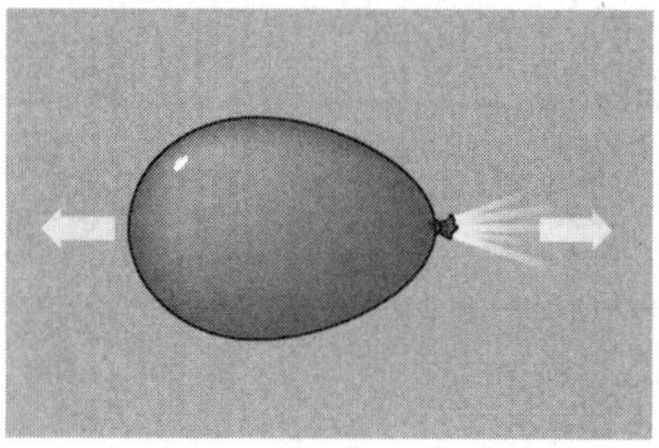

    _____

    _____

    _____ [2 marks]

b What is the total momentum of the balloon before he lets go?

    _____   [1 mark]

c Describe what happens to the total momentum after he lets go.

    _____   [1 mark]

d Use the idea of momentum to explain

    i why a swimmer moves forward in the water.

    _____

    _____   [3 marks]

B–A*

    ii why a swimmer spins in the water if they push in the same direction with both arms.

    _____

    _____   [3 marks]

Keep it safe

1 a Explain why a force affects the momentum of an object.

_____ [1 mark]

b A car seat belt is slightly elastic. If the car is in a crash, the belt stretches slightly and the passenger is less likely to be hurt.

  i What is momentum of a car that is stopped?

_____ [1 mark]

  ii The elastic in the seat belt lets the momentum of the car change over a longer time. Why does this help passengers avoid getting hurt?

_____

_____ [2 marks]

c Describe how a car's crumple zone affects the momentum change of passengers in a head-on collision.

_____

_____ [2 marks]

2 Adam drops his mobile phone onto a concrete path and it breaks. Sarah drops her mobile phone onto a carpet and it does not break.

a What is the momentum of each mobile phone after it lands?

_____ [1 mark]

b Each mobile phone has the same change in momentum.

  i Explain why Sarah's phone did not break.

_____

_____

_____ [3 marks]

  ii If the momentum of Adam's phone immediately before it landed was 1 kg m/s, and it took 0.02 s to stop, calculate the force it felt.

_____

_____ [3 marks]

Static electricity

3 Owen rubs a balloon on some cloth. The balloon becomes charged.

a What particles are negatively charged?

_____

[1 mark]

b Explain how rubbing the balloon makes it negatively charged.

_____

_____

_____ [3 marks]

c The negatively charged balloon is held near another negatively charged balloon. Describe what happens.

_____

_____ [2 marks]

Charge

D–C

1 a Explain how electrical charge behaves differently in electrical conductors and in electrical insulators.

_____

_____ [2 marks]

b Damien is rubbing a balloon with a piece of woollen cloth.
i Explain how a static charge can build up on the balloon.

_____

_____

_____ [3 marks]

B–A*

ii Explain why the charged up balloon can stick on an uncharged wall.

_____

_____

_____ [3 marks]

D–C

2 a What is a gold leaf electroscope used to detect?

_____ [1 mark]

b Explain you can use a gold leaf electroscope to compare a charged up comb and an uncharged comb.

_____

_____

_____ [3 marks]

Van de Graaff generator

D–C

3

dome

upper roller

belt

lower roller

a What type of material are the belt and rollers made of?

_____ [1 mark]

b Explain how the belt and rollers create a charge.

_____

_____ [2 marks]

c Explain why the equipment must stay on an insulated mat.

_____ [1 mark]

Sparks will fly!

1 a During a thunderstorm, clouds lose their electric charge as lightning. Many buildings have lightning conductors. Explain how a lightning conductor can protect the building during a thunderstorm.

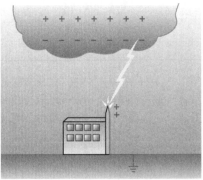

_____

_____

_____

_____

[3 marks]

D–C

b How can you tell if a charged object loses its charge suddenly?

_____ [1 mark]

c Why are structures in an oil refinery earthed?

_____

_____ [2 marks]

2 A photocopier uses static electricity to transfer negatively charged toner to a sheet of paper. First, the toner passes over a positively charged drum.

D–C

a Why does the toner stick to the drum?

_____ [1 mark]

b Paper passes over the drum and the toner sticks to the paper. What charge does the paper need to have?

_____ [1 mark]

3 When paint is sprayed from a can it becomes electrically charged.

D–C

a Explain why the paint becomes positively charged.

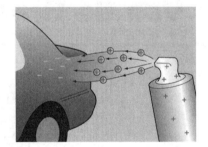

_____

_____

_____

[2 marks]

b The particles spread thinly and evenly on the car's surface. Explain why the particles spread out.

_____

_____ [2 marks]

4 Describe how a smoke precipitator uses electrostatics to reduce pollution.

B–A*

_____

_____

_____ [3 marks]

P2a revision checklist

I know:

how we can describe the way things move

☐ how to calculate the speed of a body from the slope of a distance-time graph

☐ how to calculate the acceleration of a body from the slope of a velocity-time graph

☐ how to calculate the distance travelled by a body from a velocity-time graph

how we make things speed up or slow down

☐ to change the speed of an object, an unbalanced force must act on it

☐ forces can add up or cancel out to give a resultant force; when the resultant force is *not* zero, an object accelerates:

resultant force (N) = mass × acceleration: $F = ma$

☐ an object falling through a fluid accelerates until it reaches a terminal velocity, when the resultant force is zero

☐ the stopping distance of a car is the thinking distance plus the braking distance; this increases as the speed increases

what happens to the movement energy when things speed up or slow down

☐ when a force causes an object to move, energy is transferred and work is done

☐ every moving object has kinetic energy that can be transformed into other forms

☐ the kinetic energy of a body depends on its mass and its speed:

kinetic energy $= \frac{1}{2} \times$ mass $\times$ speed^2

what momentum is

☐ every moving object has momentum that depends on its mass and its velocity:

momentum = mass × velocity

☐ momentum has size and direction and is conserved in collisions and explosions

☐ how to use the equation:

$$\text{force} = \frac{\text{change in momentum}}{\text{time taken for the change}}$$

what static electricity is, how it can be used and the connection between static electricity and electric currents

☐ rubbing electrical insulators together builds up static electricity because electrons are transferred

☐ if an object gains electrons it has a negative charge; if it loses electrons it has a positive charge

☐ electrostatic charges can be used in photocopiers, smoke precipitators and paint sprayers

☐ when electrical charges move we get an electrical current

☐ if potential difference becomes high enough, a spark may jump across the gap between a body and any earthed conductor which is brought near it

Circuit diagrams

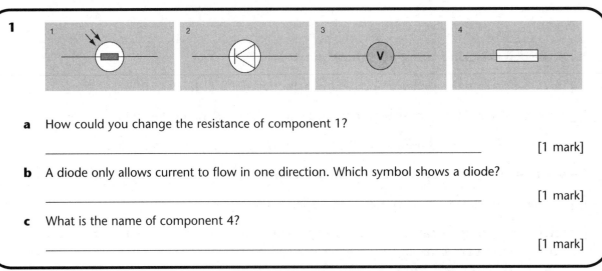

1

a How could you change the resistance of component 1?

_____

[1 mark]

b A diode only allows current to flow in one direction. Which symbol shows a diode?

_____

[1 mark]

c What is the name of component 4?

_____

[1 mark]

2 The circuit shows the wiring of a circuit in a reading lamp.

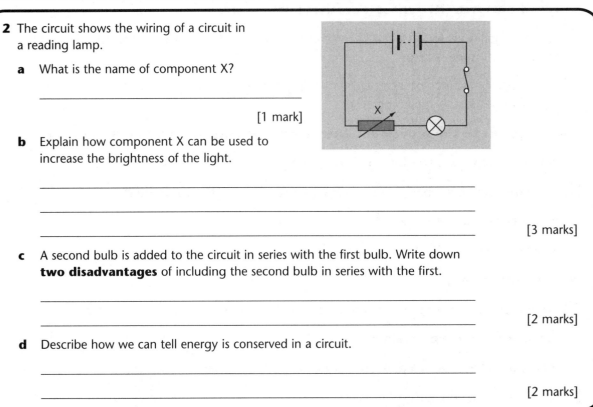

a What is the name of component X?

_____

[1 mark]

b Explain how component X can be used to increase the brightness of the light.

_____

_____

_____

[3 marks]

c A second bulb is added to the circuit in series with the first bulb. Write down **two disadvantages** of including the second bulb in series with the first.

_____

_____

[2 marks]

d Describe how we can tell energy is conserved in a circuit.

_____

_____

[2 marks]

Resistance 1

3 a What is meant by **electrical current**?

_____

_____

[2 marks]

b How is the resistance in a conductor different from the resistance in an insulator?

_____

_____

[2 marks]

c Give **one** reason why metals are better conductors of electricity than plastics.

_____

_____

[1 mark]

Resistance 2

1 a The resistance of a wire depends on collisions inside the wire. Explain what the collision theory of resistance is.

_____

_____

_____ [3 marks]

b Use this idea to explain why different materials have a different resistance.

_____ [1 mark]

Ohm's Law

2 The graph shows the results of an experiment to find out how current changes when the voltage changes in a wire.

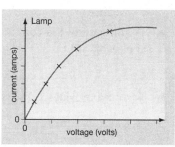

a What pattern does the graph show?

_____

_____

_____

_____ [2 marks]

b Use the graph to write down the current when the voltage is 6 V.

_____ [1 mark]

c Use your answer to part **b** to calculate the resistance of the wire at 6 V.

_____

_____

_____ [3 marks]

d The length and thickness of the wire stay the same. Write down **two** other factors to keep constant for the resistance of the wire to stay the same.

_____

_____ [2 marks]

e The graph shows the experiment repeated using a filament bulb. Write down **one** reason why this graph is a different shape from the graph in part **a**.

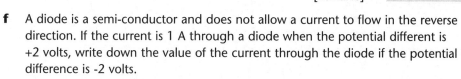

_____

_____

_____

_____ [2 marks]

f A diode is a semi-conductor and does not allow a current to flow in the reverse direction. If the current is 1 A through a diode when the potential different is +2 volts, write down the value of the current through the diode if the potential difference is -2 volts.

_____ [1 mark]

More components

1 a How could you change the resistance of the thermistor?

_____

_____

D–C

[1 mark]

b What happens inside the thermistor when it is heated up?

_____

_____

B–A*

[2 marks]

c Explain how a digital thermometer takes temperature readings.

_____

_____

[2 marks]

d How does the resistance of the light dependent resistor change if a light shines onto it?

_____

_____

D–C

[1 mark]

e Explain how automatic lighting systems are designed to switch off at night.

_____

_____

B–A*

[2 marks]

Components in series

2 The circuit shows three bulbs wired in series.

D–C

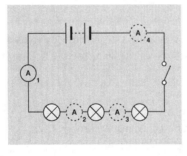

a Fred measures the current in four places in the circuit. What can you say about the readings?

_____

[1 mark]

b Each cell provides 1.5 V. What is the size of the voltage supplied to the circuit?

_____

[1 mark]

c Write down the voltage across each of the three bulbs.

1_____ 2_____ 3_____

[1 mark]

d If the number of bulbs in the circuit doubles, how does the resistance of the circuit change?

_____

[1 mark]

Components in parallel

1 The circuit shows three bulbs wired in parallel. The circuit is switched on.

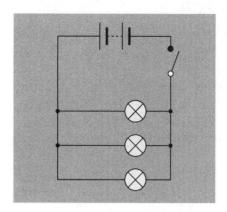

a If the current through each bulb is 0.5 A, how big is the current through the battery?

_____ [1 mark]

b Each cell provides 1.5 V. What is the size of the voltage supplied to the circuit?

_____ [1 mark]

c Write down the voltage across each of the three bulbs.

_____ [1 mark]

d Write down **one** reason to wire the bulbs in parallel rather than in series.

_____ [1 mark]

The three-pin plug

2 The diagram shows a plug connecting the lead from an iron.

a Why are the cable and casing made of plastic?

_____

_____ [1 mark]

b Explain why the fuse must be connected in series to the live wire.

_____

_____

_____

_____ [2 marks]

c Describe the structure of the cable that connects the plug to the equipment.

_____

_____

_____ [3 marks]

d Explain why a radio does not need to be earthed but is still safe to use.

_____

_____ [2 marks]

Domestic electricity

1   X   Y

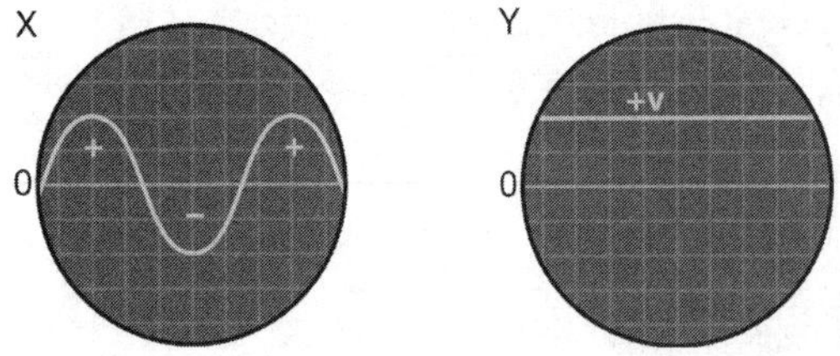

a   Which diagram shows the trace you would get from a battery?

_____   [1 mark]

b   Explain what is meant by the phrase 'the frequency of the current is 50 Hz'.

_____

_____   [2 marks]

c   What equipment is used to show the picture of changing voltage in a circuit?

_____   [1 mark]

d   Describe how the potential difference of mains supply changes through one cycle.

_____

_____

_____   [3 marks]

D–C

B–A*

Safety at home

2 Brad's radio stopped working until his dad changed the fuse for him.

a   How does the fuse protect the radio from damage?

_____

_____

_____   [2 marks]

b   Why is a different fuse needed for Brad's electric heater?

_____   [1 mark]

c   Explain why Brad's electric heater needs to be earthed but his radio does not.

_____   [1 mark]

d   Explain how earthing the heater protects the user.

_____

_____

_____   [3 marks]

e   Explain why a circuit breaker is safer to use than a fuse.

_____

_____   [2 marks]

D–C

Which fuse?

1 a Nathan has to put a fuse into a plug for a radio. He has a choice of fuses rated at 3 A, 5 A or 13 A. The current flowing through the radio is 0.4 A.

   i Which fuse should he use?

_____ [1 mark]

   ii One fuse has '13 A' printed on it. What does this tell you about the fuse?

_____

_____ [3 marks]

b **i** Nathan also has a heater. Its power rating is 2000 W. Calculate the size of the current flowing through the heater, if mains electricity is supplied at 230 V.

_____ A [3 marks]

   ii What would happen if Nathan put a fuse in with too low a rating?

_____

_____ [2 marks]

   iii Calculate the charge flowing through the heater each second. The voltage of mains supply is 230 V. Include units in your answer.

_____

_____ [3 marks]

Radioactivity

2 a **i** In an atom, which particle has no charge?

_____ [1 mark]

   ii In an atom, which particles are found in the nucleus?

_____ [2 marks]

b What is an ion?

_____ [1 mark]

c This table gives information about different atoms.

   i Write down the mass number for beryllium.

_____ [1 mark]

   ii How many protons has boron got in its nucleus?

_____ [1 mark]

   iii How many neutrons has helium got in its nucleus?

_____ [1 mark]

Element	Atomic No.	Notation
Hydrogen	1	^1_1H
Helium	2	^4_2He
Lithium	3	^7_3Li
Beryllium	4	^9_4Be
Boron	5	$^{11}_5B$
Carbon	6	$^{12}_6C$

d Carbon has several isotopes.

   i What is different for different isotopes of carbon?

_____ [1 mark]

   ii What is the same for all isotopes of carbon?

_____ [1 mark]

Alpha, beta and gamma rays 2

1 a What is meant by the term

   i unstable _____ [1 mark]

   ii radioisotope _____ [1 mark]

b Alpha radiation is the most **ionising** type of radiation. Explain what ionising means.

_____

_____ [2 marks]

c Explain why gamma rays can travel further in air than alpha particles.

_____

_____ [2 marks]

d Americium-241 decays by losing an alpha particle, forming a new element.
Complete the values of X and Y in this equation.

$$^{241}_{X}Am \rightarrow ^{Y}_{93}Np + ^{4}_{2}\alpha$$

X = _____

Y = _____ [2 marks]

Background radiation 2

2 The diagram shows the main sources of background radiation.

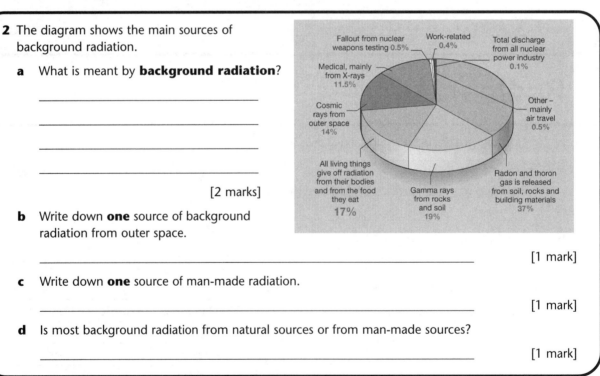

a What is meant by **background radiation**?

_____

_____

_____

_____

[2 marks]

b Write down **one** source of background radiation from outer space.

_____ [1 mark]

c Write down **one** source of man-made radiation.

_____ [1 mark]

d Is most background radiation from natural sources or from man-made sources?

_____ [1 mark]

3 Radon gas is radioactive and comes from rocks like granite.

a Why do some parts of the United Kingdom have a higher background radioactivity than others?

_____ [2 marks]

b Explain whether we should allow people to live in places where there is granite rock.

_____

_____

_____ [3 marks]

Inside the atom

1 The diagram shows one of the first models of the atom.

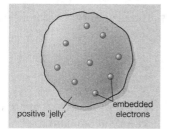

positive 'jelly'   embedded electrons

a Write down the three main features of the nuclear model of the atom.

_____

_____

_____ [3 marks]

b What evidence is there that inside an atom
  i there is a positively charged nucleus?

_____

[1 mark]

  ii the nucleus is very small?

_____

[1 mark]

  iii electrons orbit outside the nucleus?

_____

[1 mark]

c Describe how different forces interact in the nucleus.

_____

_____

[3 marks]

Nuclear fission

2 a What is **nuclear fission**?

_____

_____

[2 marks]

b Write down **one** use for nuclear fission.

_____

[1 mark]

c The picture shows a chain reaction.
  i How many neutrons are produced from each reaction?

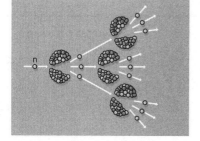

_____

_____

[1 mark]

  ii Why does a chain reaction make the size of the reaction increase?

_____

_____

[2 marks]

d Explain why only certain elements can undergo fission.

_____

_____

[2 marks]

e This equation shows one stage in a chain reaction.

$$^{235}_{92}U + 10n \rightarrow {}^{144}_{56}Ba + {}^{90}_{36}Kr + {}^{1}_{0}n + {}^{1}_{0}n + \textbf{ENERGY}$$

Explain why this chain reaction will involve more atoms at each stage.

_____

[1 mark]

Nuclear power station

1 The diagram shows a nuclear power station.

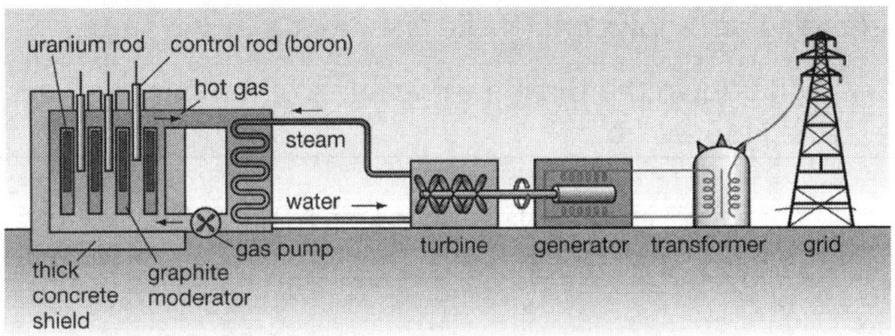

uranium rod   control rod (boron)
hot gas
steam
water →
gas pump   turbine   generator   transformer   grid
thick concrete shield   graphite moderator

a What type of reaction takes place in the uranium rod?

_____ [1 mark]

b How are the nuclear reactions controlled?

_____

_____ [2 marks]

c What energy change takes place in the generator?

_____ [1 mark]

d How does the nuclear reactor
i create steam?

_____

_____

_____ [3 marks]

ii generate electricity?

_____

_____ [2 marks]

e Describe what happens to the spent nuclear fuel.

_____

_____ [2 marks]

D–C

B–A*

Nuclear fusion

2 a What is **nuclear fusion**?

_____

_____ [2 marks]

b Write down **one** place where nuclear fusion takes place.

_____ [1 mark]

c One nuclear fusion reaction involves hydrogen nuclei. What is created when hydrogen nuclei fuse?

_____

_____ [2 marks]

d Why are large amounts of heat and pressure needed for nuclear fusion to take place?

_____

_____ [2 marks]

e Describe **two** difficulties when trying to recreate nuclear fusion to generate electricity.

_____

_____ [2 marks]

D–C

B–A*

P2b revision checklist

I know:

what the current through an electrical current depends on

☐ the symbols for components shown in circuit diagrams

☐ resistance is increased in long, thin, heated wires

☐ the current through a component depends on its resistance; the greater the resistance the smaller the current for a given p.d. across the component

    potential difference   =   current   ×   resistance

☐ in a series circuit: the total resistance is the sum of the resistance of each component; the current is the same through each component; the total p.d. of the supply is shared between the components

☐ in a parallel circuit: the total current through the whole circuit is the sum of the currents through the separate components; the p.d. across each component is the same

what mains electricity is and how it can be used safely

☐ mains electricity is an a.c. supply of 230 V and has a frequency of 50 Hz; it is very dangerous

☐ fuses and earth wires protect appliances from damage and people from harm

☐ three-pin plugs must be wired correctly and hold the correct fuse

☐ how to interpret diagrams of oscilloscope traces

why we need to know the power of electrical appliances

☐ the power of an electrical appliance is the rate at which it transforms energy:

$$\text{power} = \frac{\text{energy transformed}}{\text{time taken}}$$

☐ **energy transformed   =   potential difference   ×   charge**
   charge   =   current   ×   time

☐ most appliances have their power and the p.d. of the supply they need printed on them so we can calculate the current and fuse required

what happens to radioactive substances when they decay

☐ isotopes (elements with the same number of protons but a different number of neutrons) with unstable nuclei emit energy as radiation

☐ how the Rutherford and Marsden scattering experiment revealed the structure of the atom

☐ background radiation comes from rocks, soil, cosmic rays, living things and medical X-rays

what nuclear fission and nuclear fusion are

☐ nuclear fission is the splitting of an atomic nucleus; it is used in nuclear reactors

☐ nuclear fusion is the joining of two smaller nuclei to form a larger one; stars release energy by nuclear fusion

Periodic table

Key

relative atomic mass	atomic symbol	name	atomic (proton) number
1	H	hydrogen	1

Group 1

| 7 Li lithium 3 |
| 23 Na sodium 11 |
| 39 K potassium 19 |
| 85 Rb rubidium 37 |
| 133 Cs caesium 55 |
| [223] Fr francium 87 |

Group 2

| 9 Be beryllium 4 |
| 24 Mg magnesium 12 |
| 40 Ca calcium 20 |
| 88 Sr strontium 38 |
| 137 Ba barium 56 |
| [226] Ra radium 88 |

Transition elements

45 Sc scandium 21	48 Ti titanium 22	51 V vanadium 23	52 Cr chromium 24	55 Mn manganese 25	56 Fe iron 26	59 Co cobalt 27	59 Ni nickel 28	63.5 Cu copper 29	65 Zn zinc 30
89 Y yttrium 39	91 Zr zirconium 40	93 Nb niobium 41	96 Mo molybdenum 42	[98] Tc technetium 43	101 Ru ruthenium 44	103 Rh rhodium 45	106 Pd palladium 46	108 Ag silver 47	112 Cd cadmium 48
139 La* lanthanum 57	178 Hf hafnium 72	181 Ta tantalum 73	184 W tungsten 74	186 Re rhenium 75	190 Os osmium 76	192 Ir iridium 77	195 Pt platinum 78	197 Au gold 79	201 Hg mercury 80
[227] Ac* actinium 89	[261] Rf rutherfordium 104	[262] Db dubnium 105	[266] Sg seaborgium 106	[264] Bh bohrium 107	[277] Hs hassium 108	[268] Mt meitnerium 109	[271] Ds darmstadtium 110	[272] Rg roentgenium 111	

Groups 3–8

3	4	5	6	7	8
					4 He helium 2
11 B boron 5	12 C carbon 6	14 N nitrogen 7	16 O oxygen 8	19 F fluorine 9	20 Ne neon 10
27 Al aluminium 13	28 Si silicon 14	31 P phosphorus 15	32 S sulfur 16	35.5 Cl chlorine 17	40 Ar argon 18
70 Ga gallium 31	73 Ge germanium 32	75 As arsenic 33	79 Se selenium 34	80 Br bromine 35	84 Kr krypton 36
115 In indium 49	119 Sn tin 50	122 Sb antimony 51	128 Te tellurium 52	127 I iodine 53	131 Xe xenon 54
204 Tl thallium 81	207 Pb lead 82	209 Bi bismuth 83	[209] Po polonium 84	[210] At astatine 85	[222] Rn radon 86

Elements with atomic numbers 112–116 have been reported but not fully authenticated.

* The Lanthanides (atomic numbers 58–71) and the Actinides (atomic numbers 90–103) have been omitted.
Cu and Cl have not been rounded to the nearest whole number.